T0113941

Praise for *Love Has Forgotten No One*

"No, I won't give away any details here and spoil your reading fun. As with the earlier books, it's not even those little personal details that make it an exciting read. They are just glitter. So, if not for the news items, why are we eager for more? The truth, for his growing body of steady readers, is that Gary has agreed to share his life with us, warts and all, and enables us to learn A Course in Miracles *with him, in a fun and intense way, always going deeper and deeper into its experiential implications. The comedy of his life invites us to increasingly realize what the* Course *is actually saying."*

— **Rogier Fentener van Vlissingen,** author of *Closing the Circle: Pursah's Gospel of Thomas and* A Course in Miracles

*"****Love Has Forgotten No One*** *is not really a book—rather, it's a portal, a transport system, a rearranging of the mind. When you've finished reading it, I believe you'll be closer to knowing your True Nature. All that, and Gary's funny, too!"*

— **H. Ronald Hulnick, Ph.D.,** President, University of Santa Monica; co-author with Mary R. Hulnick, Ph.D., of *Loyalty to Your Soul: The Heart of Spiritual Psychology*

LOVE

Has Forgotten No One

ALSO BY GARY R. RENARD

THE DISAPPEARANCE OF THE UNIVERSE:
Straight Talk about Illusions, Past Lives, Religion,
Sex, Politics, and the Miracles of Forgiveness

YOUR IMMORTAL REALITY:
How to Break the Cycle of Birth and Death

ENLIGHTENMENT CARDS:
Thoughts from The Disappearance of the Universe (a 72-card deck)

All of the above are available at your local bookstore,
or may be ordered by visiting:

Hay House USA: www.hayhouse.com®
Hay House Australia: www.hayhouse.com.au
Hay House UK: www.hayhouse.co.uk
Hay House India: www.hayhouse.co.in

LOVE
Has Forgotten No One
THE ANSWER TO LIFE

GARY R. RENARD

HAY HOUSE, INC.
Carlsbad, California • New York City
London • Sydney • New Delhi

Published in the United States by: Hay House, Inc.: www.hayhouse.com®
Published in Australia by: Hay House Australia Pty. Ltd.: www.hayhouse.com.au
Published in the United Kingdom by: Hay House UK, Ltd.: www.hayhouse.co.uk
Published in India by: Hay House Publishers India: www.hayhouse.co.in

Cover design: Amy Rose Grigoriou • *Interior design:* Riann Bender

Library of Congress Cataloging-in-Publication Data

Renard, Gary R.
Love has forgotten no one : the answer to life / Gary R. Renard. -- 1st edition.
    pages cm
ISBN 978-1-4019-1723-4 (alk. paper)
1. Course in Miracles. 2. Spiritual life. 3. Spirituality. I. Title.
BP605.C68R475 2013
299'.93--dc23
                                                2013010969

Tradepaper ISBN: 978-1-4019-1724-1

1st edition, October 2013
2nd edition, October 2014

For Karen L. Renard
Thank you for helping me through life.

CONTENTS

INTRODUCTION

This is a book about spirituality, *real* spirituality, not what has been passing for spirituality in the pop media over the last two decades. Spirituality has become totally confused with the self-help movement. By the time you finish this book, you'll not only know the difference between the two, but you'll also know why only one of them will ever make you happy.

There's a difference between a spirituality that will save you a lot of time and spiritualities that won't. Those that save you time will introduce you to the idea of *undoing the ego* and show you how to do it. The "ego" is something that great teachings, such as Buddhism and the spiritual masterpiece *A Course in Miracles,* define in detail and also describe in strikingly similar ways. In fact, you'll find that there are more similarities between Buddhism and *A Course in Miracles* than there are between Christianity and *A Course in Miracles,* even though the *Course* uses Christian terminology to speak to a Western audience.

Without going into the distinctions and applications that are necessary to undo the ego, which will come later, let's say for now that the ego is the idea and experience that somehow we have separated ourselves from our Source; that there's this thing that has taken on a personal existence, an identity of its own, that is *not* one with its source, and we believe it is real. The focus of accelerated spiritual discipline is to undo this ego, which is based on the idea of separation.

If you undid the false you, which is the ego, then the real you would be all that's left. You don't have to struggle to be the real you. You do not have to evolve. The real you is *already* perfect. What needs to be done is to remove the barriers to the experience and the expression of that perfection. Incidentally, that perfection has nothing to do with anything in this world, but something that is not of this world.

There are people, including obviously brilliant and revered scientists, who will teach you that you should "make friends with your ego." That's cute. The only problem is that your ego is not interested in being your friend. Your ego wants to kill you. As *A Course in Miracles*—which was dictated by Jesus (who is referred to in this book as "J") to research psychologist Helen Schucman—puts it: "The ego is, therefore, particularly likely to attack you when you react lovingly, because it has evaluated you as unloving and you are going against its judgment. The ego will attack your motives as soon as they become clearly out of accord with its perception of you. This is when it will shift abruptly from suspiciousness to viciousness, since its uncertainty is increased."[1]

This is not a book about trying to make spiritual what cannot be made spiritual. It's a book about going home to spirit. It's about reality. That reality is love, but certainly not love in the way in which the world traditionally thinks of it. This is a love that cannot be explained, only experienced. It's the goal that the great mystics throughout history have wisely pointed us toward, but knew it could not be described. Still, it's possible to experience this reality even while we appear to be here as bodies. We are *not* bodies, but it does look and feel like we are. It's not my purpose to deny people their experience that they are bodies. It's simply my purpose to demonstrate that this is a *false* experience.

This is also true of our experience of time. We experience time as linear and that we're making all of this up as we go along. That's also a false experience. The truth is holographic. It all already happened. And if it all already happened, then you can't be making it up as you go along. You don't get to create the way that it is. You already did that at the beginning of time. Everything that appeared to happen after that was already a done deal. Most people don't like that idea, yet that idea is part of a thought system that, if they were to understand and apply it, could save them an incredible amount of time within their illusory experience.

We won't always have a choice as to what we experience, but we will always have a choice as to *how* we experience it. The essence of that choice lies in a certain kind of forgiveness; the same kind of forgiveness that was practiced by great masters such as Buddha and Jesus. This is also not the kind of forgiveness that the world traditionally thinks of. But once we learn it, and do it, it *undoes* the ego and leads us back to our true home, which is one with our Source. This is spiritual life in the fast lane, because it saves time—a great deal of time. It saves countless lifetimes, too, which are actually serial dreams, but which we take as reality. The answer to life is to replace the false experience of being a seemingly separate being, a spatial being, with the true experience of being perfect Spirit, which is not just nonspatial, but beyond the universe of time and space altogether. It's the experience that great spirituality is directed toward, which literally is the answer to life and its most difficult questions.

To get to this experience of reality, which is perfect oneness with God, requires noncompromise. This book doesn't compromise on the teachings of the *Course* because my teachers refuse to compromise on those teachings, and so must I. As the *Course* bluntly puts it on page 66 of the Manual for Teachers: "The world attempts a thousand compromises, and will attempt a thousand more. Not one can be acceptable to God's teachers, because not one could be acceptable to God."

In that spirit, the following text relates true events that occurred from the end of 2006 through the beginning of 2013. Except for my narration and notes, they are presented within the framework of a dialogue that has three participants: **Gary** (that's me) and **Arten** and **Pursah**, two ascended masters who appeared to me in the flesh. My narration is not labeled unless it interrupts the dialogue, in which case it is simply labeled "NOTE." The many italicized words you will see indicate an emphasis on the part of the speakers.

It is not absolutely essential to believe that the appearances of the ascended masters took place in order to derive benefits from the information in these chapters, and I personally don't care what you think. However, I can vouch for the extreme unlikeliness of this writing being done by an uneducated layman such as myself without inspiration from these teachers. At any rate, I leave it up to you, the reader, to think whatever you choose about the book's origins.

I've made every effort to do this right, but I'm not perfect, so this book isn't perfect either. However, if there are any errors of fact in these pages, you can be certain that they are my mistakes and were not made by my visitors. Also, the reporting of these discussions, which follow an easily observable "real life" timeline, are not always linear but sometimes holographic. In just a few instances, things that were said earlier are included later in the book, and things that were said later are presented earlier. I would never make a decision about that, or anything else in regard to these books, without being guided to do so by my teachers.

References to *A Course in Miracles* (ACIM), including each chapter's introductory quotation, are noted and listed in the Index in the back of the book. Limitless gratitude goes to the Voice of the *Course,* whose true identity is discussed herein.

I want to thank four people who helped to make this book possible: my first booking agent, Sue Borg, who did such a good job that I had an opportunity to speak in public in many diverse places and still have the time to learn something from my teachers; Jan Cook, my friend and second booking agent who was nothing less than a godsend; my former wife, Karen L. Renard, who has become one of my teachers as well as a great friend; and one other person whom you will meet in these pages, revealing the identity of Arten in this lifetime.

LHFNO, as people are already calling it, contains many quotations from the official version of *A Course in Miracles,* which are noted in order to assist you, the reader, in studying the *Course* later if you choose to do so. The opening chapter quotes are italicized, even if they are not italicized in the *Course.* The publisher and I would like to express our gratitude to the members of both the

Foundation for Inner Peace in Mill Valley, California, the original publishers of the *Course,* and the Foundation for *A Course in Miracles* in Temecula, California, for their decades of important work that have resulted in making *A Course in Miracles* available to the world. Ordering information for the authentic version of the *Course* is printed in the back of this book.

Finally, although I am not affiliated with them, I would like to take this opportunity to extend my sincere thanks to Gloria Wapnick and Kenneth Wapnick, Ph.D., the founders of the Foundation for *A Course in Miracles,* upon whose work much of this book is based. I was guided very early on by Arten and Pursah to become a student of the Wapnicks' teachings, and this book cannot help but reflect all of my learning experiences.

— **Gary Renard**

basking in the glow of Southern California,
and only five hours from Hawaii

*I have stated that the basic concepts referred to in this
Course are not matters of degree. Certain fundamental
concepts cannot be understood in terms of opposites.
It is impossible to conceive of light and darkness or everything and
nothing as joint possibilities. They are all true or all false.
It is essential that you realize your thinking will be erratic
until a firm commitment to one or the other is made.* [2]

A COURSE IN MIRACLES

1

WHAT WOULD YOU RATHER BE?

---

*You are as God created you, and so is every living thing you look
upon, regardless of the images you see. What you behold
as sickness and as pain, as weakness and as suffering and loss,
is but temptation to perceive yourself defenseless and in hell.
Yield not to this, and you will see all pain, in every form,
wherever it occurs, but disappear as mists before the sun.[3]*

At the end of 2006, I was married and living in Maine. By the
end of 2007, I would be divorced and living in California. 2006
had been the wildest year of my life, yet I had no idea that 2007
would surpass it. Indeed, I wouldn't have even thought it was
possible.

I had last seen my beloved Ascended Master Teachers, Arten
and Pursah, who appeared to me as a man and a woman, in August of 2005. They had visited me 11 times over 20 months in
order to give me their share of the material for our second book,
Your Immortal Reality: How to Break the Cycle of Birth and Death.
(I supplied my narration and notes, and kept up my end of the
conversations the best I could.) Toward the end of their final visit,
I asked if I'd ever see them again. Their answer took me by surprise:

A year from now, think about whether or not the kind of life you're living is really what you want. Do you want to keep being an author?

They knew something I didn't. The next year and few months would be very hard. In the middle of a travel and speaking schedule that would severely test anyone, and while attempting to do all the other work an active author does, I became the target of a vendetta—a jealous and organized personal campaign from so-called spiritual teachers who got together in an attempt to destroy my ministry.

One of them was a man who I thought was my friend and for whom I had done numerous favors. It hurt badly, and it was one of the biggest forgiveness lessons of my life. It took me several months to work through the situation. Fortunately for me, the efforts of these few individuals failed, probably because what they were doing was diametrically opposed to everything that the spiritual principles they were supposedly teaching stood for. People don't like hypocrisy. These teachers paid lip service to love and smelled of sour grapes.

As for me, I was simply my known imperfect self. I had made myself so available to the public that people felt they knew me. I had never presented myself as being anything but human. Both my personality and my story had remained consistent and uncompromising despite years of vicious scrutiny. There was no evidence to support the hatred being leveled at me, except for opinions. Those opinions would be demonstrated to be an extreme minority. At the end of the day, most of the people were with me, and this would be proven many times in the months and years to come.

About a year after Arten and Pursah's last visit of the second series, I was leading an intensive workshop at the Omega Institute in Rhinebeck, New York. A great guy named Joe, who was a Vietnam veteran, told me how the book *The Disappearance of the Universe* (or "D.U.," as it's affectionately called by many of its readers) had led him to *A Course in Miracles*. Because of D.U., Joe was able to understand and apply the *Course's* teachings to his life. That in turn had empowered him to be able to forgive the horrific things he saw in Vietnam. It also put an end to the decades of nightmares that had followed. Joe said he wanted to share the book with other Vietnam vets. It was at that instant that my answer to Arten and Pursah's question became a no-brainer. *Yes, of course I want to continue this work. What more could I ask for?*

A few months later, after dealing with the attempted attacks by the other teachers, I found myself in the living room of my apartment in Auburn, Maine. It was December 21, 2006, and I had a good idea of what was about to happen. As one personal crisis in my life was resolved and another was about to begin, I was anticipating a visit from my friends. The ascended masters had said it should be my decision as to whether they'd appear to me again. They wanted it to be my responsibility. They had taught me to be at cause and not effect, and they expected me to live it—and to never again be a victim of the world. This time the choice was mine, and I knew they'd be there for me if I wanted them to. I wasn't disappointed. Suddenly, Arten and Pursah appeared to me on their favorite couch, which I would soon lose in my divorce, only to have my former wife give it back to me.

GARY: I knew you'd come today! And other people have been e-mailing me saying they thought you were gonna appear today.

ARTEN: Is there no escaping our fame?

PURSAH: Is the paparazzi outside? But seriously, this has been a very challenging time for you.

GARY: No kidding. Would you care to explain why you didn't warn me that I'd be subjected to more BS than any other teacher in the history of *A Course in Miracles?*

ARTEN: Excuse me, but didn't we tell you right from the start that we weren't going to tell you too much about your personal future, because we didn't want to deprive you of your forgiveness opportunities?

GARY: Oh, I forgot. Never mind. But Jesus Christ, it wasn't easy, you know.

PURSAH: Now Gary, don't talk to Jesus about easy. He went all the way, and you're well on your way. Jesus demonstrated that nothing is impossible with God, including the complete absence of pain. You've done well with your recent forgiveness work, despite your complaining here, so why don't you just be like a duck?

GARY: Okay, I'll bite. What does that mean?

ARTEN: A duck doesn't look behind itself. It's hard for a duck to do that, so it usually doesn't bother. It just sees what's right in front of its face and ignores what's behind it. All that matters is what's up right now. There's no thinking about the past.

GARY: You're saying the past should be out of my awareness— that all I should be thinking of is what there is to deal with at the present moment. Then the future will take care of itself.

ARTEN: Yes, but we're not talking about leaving it at that, like some of the popular spiritual teachings do. Any attempt to remain in the present moment will fail unless certain work is done by the student. That's because there is something in the mind that prevents you from *staying* in the present moment. Most spiritualities don't even know about it, much less teach you how to have it healed. Also, the most popular teachers of the *Course* don't know about it or teach you how to have it healed, because they haven't really learned the *Course*.

PURSAH: We'll be dealing with it to such an extent that you'll never be the same.

ARTEN: As J, the master, says in his *Course,* "The one wholly true thought one can hold about the past is that it is not here."[4]

GARY: Cool. But in the illusion of time, how long will you be coming in this series of visits? I have a heavy schedule, you know. If you're gonna take up certain dates, I have to call my agent.

ARTEN: Actually, how long we'll be coming depends on how well and how fast you do your work. We're going to be challenging you. With all your travels, you may not be able to keep up with those challenges. But your forgiveness process should be getting shorter. You noticed during the last series of visits that the advanced forgiveness processes were shorter. They'll be short this time, too. Eventually, you won't need words at all and will just do it automatically. That's a very advanced state. For now, let's say you're going to learn quickly, and in the not-too-distant future you'll learn to forgive *automatically* whatever comes up in front of your face. You'll be left in a state that will include faithfulness and joy, which are characteristics of a teacher of God.[5] You'll be in a condition of gratitude to your Creator, who did not create you to be a body, but to be like your Creator. You'll get to where you'll be able to relax in God.

GARY: Yeah, I'd like to be more relaxed and grateful for all the things that have helped me the last couple of years; you know, like J, the *Course*, you, Pursah, Just For Men, Viagra . . .

PURSAH: And you should be grateful to the people who have challenged you the last few months. By forgiving them, they have become your saviors.

GARY: Well, one of them has come around and even apologized to me in public. But I doubt if those other two jerks will ever get their heads out of their butts. Just kidding. Anything's possible. But I know exactly what you're saying. By forgiving them, I'm actually the one who is forgiven, and in that sense they really are my saviors. I couldn't get home without them.

PURSAH: That's it, dear brother. How you see them, or think of them, will determine how you think of yourself, and ultimately what you believe you are: a body or spirit. And what would you rather be? Something temporary that is doomed to die or something permanent that *cannot* die? And which experience you'll have is determined by how you think of others! As J counsels you in the *Course*, "Never forget this, for in him you will find yourself or lose yourself."[6]

> The kind of forgiveness we're talking about, which undoes your ego, will allow you to *stay* in the condition of the endless present.

GARY: And by forgiving whatever comes up, plus any memories or thoughts from the past that come into my mind, I'm free of it. But it's a certain kind of forgiveness that J used that's not really understood by most people.

ARTEN: The kind of forgiveness we're talking about, which undoes your ego, will allow you to *stay* in the condition of the endless present. The past and future will be forgiven. And as the *Course* says, ". . . if it is forgiven it is gone."[7]

GARY: Hey, wait! I haven't put on the tape recorder.

ARTEN: Don't worry about that. We don't want you to record this time. You can take notes, as you've already started to, and you have a great memory. Plus you can hear us very well now when we talk to you in between visits, or show you the words visibly when your eyes are closed. So we'll correct you if you make a writing mistake that's important enough to fix.

GARY: I don't know, man. It sounds harder than what I'm used to. I mean, I add my narration and notes to the books and make them mine by telling people what was going on in my life. I give a lot of personal experiences that way. But it's been a real help to me to be able to type out the actual conversations from the tapes. Now you're telling me I can't do that.

PURSAH: We're telling you that you don't have to do that. It will be okay. You'll see.

GARY: Why no tapes?

PURSAH: Simple. Because of your decision to continue with this work, it means there are going to be more books. So let's put away any questions people ask about tapes. You can do the job without tapes now. And people should concentrate on what we have to say, not superficial things like are we real or are the tapes real, when we've been trying to teach them all along that *nothing* is real except for God, including them!

Also, you've done a decent job of answering questions. People have been raising questions about you and Arten and me for years now, and you've answered all of them, just as we advised you to.

NOTE: Ever since the first series of visits ended in late 2001, I've been able to hear Arten and Pursah speak to me as the Holy Spirit, although this form of communication was not always the same as most people think. Even though I would often hear an audible Voice, most of the time the communication took another form, especially after the second book. With my eyes closed but still awake, whether sitting up or lying down in bed just before going to sleep, or upon awakening, I would see words as if I were reading a book. This is among the clearest forms of inspired communication I've received to date.

ARTEN: There's nothing wrong with answering questions, and there's nothing defensive about it either. You're just giving information in order to correct misinformation. Isn't it funny that some people think it's all right for them to attack you in the form of questions that are actually statements—that accuse you of being a liar with no evidence—yet somehow they want to make it look like there's something wrong with you if you answer them! How *convenient* for them. The truth is that on the level of form, if you don't give people your experience, then they'll just make up their own answers.

There's another reason we counseled you to answer questions. Forty or fifty years from now, when scholars look back on the issues of the day with less emotion than what many people display now, they'll see that you had answers to these questions, and usually very good answers.

PURSAH: You've become a widely known teacher around the world the last few years. Why don't you tell us, as a review for your readers, a couple of the highlights regarding what J was teaching 2,000 years ago—and is *still* teaching in *A Course in Miracles,* which the world didn't understand then, except for a few, and which the world still doesn't understand today, except for a few.

GARY: Sure, but I'll try to be brief, because I have a few questions for *you.* So, the first thing you gotta understand is that there are only two things, and that only one of them is real. What's *real* is God or Heaven or your Source or Home or reality or whatever you wanna call it. But no matter what you call it, it's perfect. As *both* the Bible and *A Course in Miracles* put it: God is perfect Love. Now this perfect love is not shifting or changing. It's absolute stillness. If it were shifting or changing, it would be evolving; and if it were evolving, it wouldn't be perfect. But reality is *already* perfect; it doesn't have to improve itself. And this is everyone's reality. This perfect love cannot be taught or explained, but it can be experienced, even when we appear to be here in a body.

Now, if God is perfect love, then all it would know how to do would be to love. If it knew how to do anything else, then it wouldn't *be* perfect love, would it? That's an important point when it comes to understanding the nondualistic nature of the *Course.*

But then there's this other thing that thinks it's here. It's not really here, but it thinks it is. This thing thinks it has separated itself from its Source and has taken on an individual identity of its own. We'll call that the ego. And the ego is mostly unconscious. It's underneath the surface. We see only a small part of it with the conscious mind, and most of it is hidden from us. And in the part that's hidden, there's this tremendous guilt over seeming to separate from God. That's what you might call the original sin— not that there's *really* any sin, but it's the idea of being separate. That made consciousness, because in order to have consciousness you've gotta have more than one thing: a subject and an object. Then you have something else to be conscious of. In reality, there is no subject or object, just perfect oneness.

So to make a long story short, you don't have to struggle to be what you already are. The real you is already perfect and change-less. All you need to do is *undo* the false you that thinks it has sep-arated itself from its Source—the false you that believes it is guilty.

PURSAH: And if God is pure, absolute perfect love, then how could there ever be this thought of separation in the first place?

GARY: Aha! That's a trick question. *A Course in Miracles* is teaching that the full awareness of the Atonement "is the recogni-tion that *the separation never occurred.*"[8]

In other words, the separation is a delusion, a dream, a projec-tion of a universe of time and space. And the answer to that delu-sion cannot be found on our own with just our intellect, which the ego often uses to keep us seemingly stuck here. The separation is a false experience. And the *real* answer to the separation is to replace it with a *true* experience, which is the awareness of perfect oneness with God. In that condition, you are no longer a separate being, but one with all creation, and that experience *is* the Answer to what we call life. In fact, in that experience there are no ques-tions, only the Answer. Then you temporarily return here to the false experience of separation, and it turns out you were dreaming the questions! Because the questions don't exist in reality, which is the experience of perfect love that is one with our Source, and which becomes our permanent reality once we lay the body aside for the final time.

PURSAH: Okay, brother. And how does one go about producing this experience?

GARY: Well, the first thing you gotta do is stop being a victim. For example, if this world was made by God, then you would be a victim of God. You would be the victim of a force that is outside of you that did it to you. But the world was not made by God, and as one of the early Workbook lessons in the *Course* puts it: "I am not a victim of the world I see."[9] By the way, that's why it's so important to understand the Text of the *Course,* or else you won't really understand the Workbook. People put their own interpretations onto the Workbook lessons, usually giving them a typical New Age spin. But the *Course* isn't New Age—it's unique. It's not teaching the same thing as the popular spiritual teachers of today. And as it says right at the beginning of the Workbook: "A theoretical foundation such as the text provides is necessary as a framework to make the exercises in this workbook meaningful.[10] Most of the *Course*'s teachers haven't really learned it and don't truly understand its meaning. Or if they do, they're certainly not telling anybody.

Most spiritual systems try to balance body, mind, and spirit. They're all equally important, but that's not the approach of the *Course.* With the *Course,* you learn how to use the mind to choose *between* the body, which is the great separation symbol of the ego and spirit, which in the *Course* is perfect oneness, not to be confused with the idea of an individual soul, which is still a separation idea.

The *Course* teaches that the world is a projection that is coming from our own collective unconscious mind. What was in our mind on a massive metaphysical level—namely the terrible unconscious guilt we felt over the initial separation from our Source—was denied and projected outward.

A psychologist will tell you that projection always follows denial. That's because when you deny something, it has to go somewhere. Now once something is denied, it becomes unconscious, and the *Course* speaks volumes about denial. So you forget that you denied it, and then when it's projected outward, you think the projection you're looking at is reality. You forget that you made it, because it's been denied! So it's your projection, but you're not aware of that. And then the *Course* teaches that "projection makes perception."[11] That means you actually made what you're looking at, but then you forgot, and you take it as reality. You forget that it's a miscreation of your own making. As J puts it, "Is it not strange that you believe to think you made the world you see is arrogance? God made it not. Of this you can be sure. What can He know of the ephemeral, the sinful and the guilty, the afraid, the suffering and lonely, and the mind that lives within a body that must die? You but accuse Him of insanity, to think He made a world where such things seem to have reality. He is not mad. Yet only madness makes a world like this."[12]

ARTEN: You and your friend J have got to stop holding things back. So you've said part of the way out is to stop being a victim and obviously take responsibility for your experience. Would you like to be a little more specific about how to do that?

GARY: Well, you can't do it through clever thinking or by being your own teacher. You need to listen to the Holy Spirit's thought system instead of your own. The truth is simple and consistent, but the ego isn't. The ego is very complicated and actually *wants* the idea of separation to survive, because it makes it feel special. Then in this world it makes special relationships, which are either special love or special hate relationships, and I'm sure we'll get into that. The point is the ego loves complications because they're smoke screens over the one real problem and the one real solution.

The one real problem is the idea that we've separated ourselves from God, and the one real solution is to undo the idea of separation and go home. In order to lead us home, the Holy Spirit gives us the simple truth in the face of the ego's complexities. But the ego won't quit. It's like the Terminator—it just keeps coming. But the truth that undoes the ego will win in the long run, because the Holy Spirit is perfect, and the ego isn't.

It's possible for anyone to understand and apply the Holy Spirit's teachings. The *Course* says it's *simple,* and it doesn't just say it once. It uses the word 158 times! I looked it up in the *Concordance.* Then on top of that, the *Course* does *not* advise us or its teachers, including ascended masters, to have original ideas. In fact, it says, "Ingenious thinking is *not* the truth that shall set you free, but you are free of the need to engage in it when you are willing to let it go."[13] And it also says—wait, let me look at it here—"The Course merely gives another answer, once a question has been raised. However, this answer does not attempt to resort to inventiveness or ingenuity. These are attributes of the ego. *The Course is simple.* It has one function and one goal. Only in that does it remain wholly consistent because only that can *be* consistent."[14]

You change your experience of yourself by changing the way you look at other people.

ARTEN: That's true. But you still haven't given me the key. Based on what you've said, what is it about the *Course* that changes your experience?

GARY: You change your experience of yourself by changing the way you look at other people.

PURSAH: Precisely. Forgiveness is a change in the way of looking at things, whether it's situations, events, or other people. But it's not easy.

GARY: I never tell people it's easy to forgive other people. In fact, it sucks because they don't deserve it.

PURSAH: That may appear to be true on the level of form, but after a while you catch on to the fact that *you* are the one who's being forgiven every time you forgive others.

GARY: That's because there's really only one of us.

ARTEN: Yes. People may appear to be separate because what they're seeing is a projection that's based on the idea of separation, but that's a trick. No matter how many times the ego appears to divide, it's just an illusion. There's really only one being that thinks it has separated itself from its Source. Yes, it's *appearing* as many, but there's really always just one, and you're it. Yet the mind appears to keep dividing. Then it projects those divisions, which results in more and more people appearing to be here in the projection. But it's all smoke and mirrors. There's always just one ego no matter how many different images you see.

GARY: That would explain why you start off with just one or two people, like Adam and Eve, and somewhere down the road you appear to have billions of people. I always wondered how reincarnation would fit into that. I mean, if you only had two individuals, then how could they appear to reincarnate into billions of people unless the mind was splitting? It wouldn't be possible. And I say "appear to reincarnate" because it's all an illusion, or better yet a dream, that simply appears to be true. Yes, events in a dream do *appear* to happen, but that doesn't mean that they're *really* happening.

PURSAH: Do you believe in reincarnation?

GARY: No, but I used to in another lifetime.

ARTEN: You said you change your experience of yourself by changing the way you look at other people. We need to make a couple of distinctions here. We've quoted the *Course* before as stating a very important law of the mind: "As you see him you will see yourself."[15]

It's time to get a little more specific about that, but first, how's your hand?

NOTE: A week before A&P (as I sometimes called them in private) returned, I woke up one morning with my hand completely numb and unusable. I went to a neurologist and was diagnosed with right radial nerve damage. I was told that all my typing and constant book signings had caused this damage. The doctor said it could take up to a year to heal, if it did at all. I was determined to make sure it would heal quickly.

The symptoms happened at a good time, if there is such a thing as a good time for symptoms to appear. I had a month off for the Christmas holidays before I started traveling and speaking extensively again. I decided I wasn't going to let this affliction have an effect on me, and I had even gone on a wonderful trip to experience the Christmas season in New York City with my wife, Karen, despite the fact that I could barely use my right hand at all.

I began practicing the teachings on healing that had been given to me by both *A Course in Miracles* and my two ascended friends. The hand was improving but still hurt and was probably only at 50 percent strength on the night Arten and Pursah returned. I was taking notes the best I could, even though they sometimes looked like a child's scribble.

GARY: It's getting better. I'm doing what I've been taught.

ARTEN: Good. On our fourth visit to you in this series, we're going to talk about healing, obviously not just for you but also for your readers. You've got three weeks before you go out in the trenches again. Keep working on your hand with your mind, and then we'll talk about how you did during that fourth visit, when we'll be able to stick to the point.

PURSAH: So, back to the subject at hand . . . no pun intended. There are some basic mistakes that people make in the way they apply the *Course*. One of the reasons for that is because they don't remember what spirit really *is*. Another mistake is that they focus on illusion instead of reality.

GARY: What do you mean by that?

PURSAH: When people get into this kind of work, they often focus on the fact that life is an illusion, which is *not* the thing you want to be focusing on. That's because if it's true that as you see them you will see yourself, and it *is* true, then if you go through life seeing people and the world as an illusion, then you will eventually think of yourself in your own unconscious mind as an illusion. You'll feel empty and meaningless, which will leave you depressed. Remember, your unconscious mind will translate whatever you think about others to be a message about *you*. That's because even though you're not aware of it, your unconscious mind knows everything, including the fact that there's just one of you that thinks it's here. That's why everything you think about others is really a message from you, to you, about you. And that's how your unconscious mind will think of it. So you definitely don't want to think of people as illusions, or that's what you'll think you are, too.

It's not just students here in the U.S. who make this mistake. Because Hinduism and Buddhism have always taught that the world you see is an illusion—or impermanence, as the Buddhists put it—a lot of people in other places, including India, think of things that way. Then to compound the problem, in India they have the caste system, in which one third of the population is regarded as being less than animals. They have no rights and never will. Imagine what it does for the psyche of a nation to view a third of its people as less than human!

Fortunately, there are also many in India who practice an idea that we've borrowed from them. You see and hear it at a lot of Unity churches in this country. It's the idea of *Namaste,* which means, "The divinity in me bows down to the divinity in you." That's certainly a step in the right direction, *but,* it doesn't go far enough.

When you say, "The divinity in me bows down to the divinity in you," you're limiting that person to a tiny speck of time and space. You're making individuality real. You're also making the two of you separate, like a subject and an object. What J did was *overlook* the body. It's not that his body's eyes didn't appear to see other bodies. But he understood that he wasn't seeing with the body's eyes and that he wasn't actually in a body. He knew what he was seeing with was his mind. As he puts it in the *Course,* you are "reviewing mentally what has gone by."[16] By the way, could there be a better definition of watching a movie? It's already been filmed, and it's already over and done with. And now you're watching it. And part of what you're watching is your own body! Your body is just a part of the same projection as all those other bodies you see.

Now, instead of limiting the person you're interacting with to that tiny speck of time and space, you want to overlook the body and do what J did. You want to think of that person as being unlimited. Instead of thinking of them as being part of it, you want to think of them as being *all* of it. If you do that, it will take you away from the focus of being an illusion and result in a highly positive outcome. It will work. It will save you lifetimes of effort. If you see them as being all of it, nothing less than God, then that's how you'll eventually come to experience yourself. That's how J did it. He saw the face of Christ everywhere. In the *Course,* J is not special. He says you are his equal, and will experience that. But the way to experience it the fastest is to see the reality of spirit in everyone you encounter.

GARY: Okay. So I think of everyone I meet as being the same as God. It's the perfect oneness that the *Course* is talking about. In our natural state we're no different from God, and it's not arrogance to think that. It's arrogance to think that somehow we could be separate from God. The truth is we can't be separate from God, except in dreams, which is why you could also say that the *Course* takes the idea of the universe of time and space being an illusion and further refines it into the idea that this is a dream we will awaken from, and that awakening is enlightenment.

The key is thinking of each one as being all of it.

ARTEN: Very good. The key is thinking of each one as being all of it. If you do that you'll be doing something that very few people in history have ever done, and it will hasten your enlightenment. Your unconscious will understand that if *they* are perfect oneness with God, then it means that *you* must be perfect oneness with God. Even J had to work at this, but his vigilance eventually won out.

GARY: Man, I guess if *he* had to work at it, then everyone does.

ARTEN: Absolutely. And that brings us to what spiritual sight really is. The ego loves differences. How can you have judgment without differences? How can you have war and murder and violence without differences? So the ego wants you to think that all this separation you're seeing is true. That's what makes it real for you—your belief in it. That's what gives it its power. That's what gives it power over you. The ego craves contrasts and cons you into believing in them in the world, but the Holy Spirit sees sameness. Yes, the Holy Spirit will *contrast* its thought system with the thought system of the ego. But that is the proper use of contrast, because one is true and one is not.

The Holy Spirit doesn't think in terms of separation. It sees wholeness everywhere. And by "sees" I mean that's the way the Holy Spirit thinks. It's the way you *think* that constitutes spiritual sight. It doesn't have anything to do with the body's eyes, even though you can see symbols of spirit in the world. They're still just symbols. Reality cannot be seen with the body's eyes, but it can be experienced by the mind.

If you want to return to spirit, think like the Holy Spirit. The Holy Spirit overlooks the body, which is a false image, and thinks of the truth that is beyond the veil of illusion. This truth is perfect oneness and innocence, exactly the same as God. And thinking of other people that way *is* spiritual sight.

Now, tell us a joke.

NOTE: I had been telling jokes in my workshops for years. I found long ago that humor was an important part of my presentation. It brought comic relief to what could be some pretty heavy-duty teachings. Sometimes I'd make up a joke, or sometimes they came from others. People knew I liked jokes, and as I went around the world, they'd tell me their favorite ones. Then I got to repeat them. It was the perfect antidote to a problem that is described in the *Course:* "Into eternity, where all is one, there crept a tiny, mad idea, at which the Son of God remembered not to laugh."[17] It is okay to remember to laugh at my workshops, so we can all learn and still have a good time.

GARY: Okay. Colonel Sanders goes in to see the Pope. During the meeting he says to the Pope, "Pontiff, I've decided I'm going to make a donation of one billion dollars to the church." The Pope replies, "My, that's very generous. You must be extremely successful." But then Colonel Sanders says, "There's just one thing. You've got to change the Lord's Prayer. Instead of it saying 'Give us this day our daily bread,' it has to say 'Give us this day our daily chicken.'"

The Pope responds, "I don't know; that's a big change. I can't make a decision like that myself. I'm going to have to consult with the cardinals. We'll have to have a conference call. I'll tell you what—you come back tomorrow after I've had a chance to talk with them, and I'll give you an answer."

After Colonel Sanders leaves, the Pope calls the cardinals and says, "Okay, I've got some good news and some bad news. What do you want first, the good or the bad?" One of the cardinals says, "Give us the good news." "All right," the Pope replies, "we're about to receive a donation of one billion dollars." And all the cardinals are thrilled. But then one of the cardinals says, "Hey, wait a minute. What's the bad news?" And the Pope says, "Well, it looks like we're going to lose the Wonder Bread account."

PURSAH: Good one. Now, we should mention that there are other ways of helping to undo the ego. As you know, the big one is forgiveness, and we'll be talking more about that. But another would be to *put the Holy Spirit in charge.* That's a lot more vital than you might think, and it's not just because the Holy Spirit's judgment is better than yours. Yes, the Holy Spirit can see everything that ever happened, from the beginning of time to the end of time. But there's a more important reason. As the *Course* teaches in the Manual for Teachers, putting the Holy Spirit in charge absolves you of guilt.

When you look to a higher power than yourself for help, instead of relying on your own talents and abilities, you are actually *undoing* the idea of separation in your mind instead of reinforcing it. When you do things on your own, you're making the idea of separation stronger for yourself. But to put the Holy Spirit in charge is the way out. Take just ten seconds in the morning and say, "Holy Spirit, you be in charge of all of my thoughts and actions today." Of course what you do is a result of what you think. So the focus should be on what you think at the level of the mind, or cause, instead of on the doing, which is all effect. There isn't really cause and effect in the dream. It's all effect. The cause is the projector in the mind, and that's where the work has to be done.

Another way of undoing the ego is the original form of prayer that's talked about in The Song of Prayer pamphlet, which is no longer just a pamphlet but has been included in the third edition of *A Course in Miracles* that was recently published by The Foundation for Inner Peace. You should reread that sometime. The original form of prayer was done silently. When J used the Lord's Prayer 2,000 years ago, that wasn't the prayer. That was just an introduction, like an invocation or invitation to God. Of course the version in the Bible isn't a very good translation, plus it was changed by the church over the first few hundred years. You'll find a better version of the Lord's Prayer in the *Course,* in the Text on page 350. Would you like to read that for us?

GARY: Yeah. I've always liked that. But you're saying this is just like an introduction—a way of preparing yourself mentally to be with God. The real prayer is when you become silent and join with God in perfect oneness and get lost in God's love. It's like you're in a condition of gratitude and complete abundance, because in perfect oneness you have everything. There can't be anything missing in wholeness.

PURSAH: You've got it. So how about reading that for us, and then I'm going to ask you to read one more thing, after which we'll become silent for a few minutes and practice joining with God in perfect oneness, which is another way of undoing the separation.

GARY: Okay, here it is:

Forgive us our illusions, Father, and help us to accept our true relationship with You, in which there are no illusions, and where none can ever enter. Our holiness is Yours. What can there be in us that needs forgiveness when Yours is perfect? The sleep of forgetfulness is only the unwillingness to remember Your forgiveness and Your Love. Let us not wander into temptation, for the temptation of the Son of God is not Your Will. And let us receive only what You have given, and accept but this into the minds which You created and which You love. Amen.[18]

PURSAH: Very nice. Now read the part you like the most from The Forgotten Song. This will give a good idea of what we're going for in this meditation, as well as another good description of spiritual sight. This is the kind of experience you want as you become one with God and get lost in God's love.

GARY: Cool. Here it is:

Beyond the body, beyond the sun and stars, past everything you see and yet somehow familiar, is an arc of golden light that stretches as you look into a great and shining circle. And all the circle fills with light before your eyes. The edges of the circle disappear, and what is in it is no longer contained at all. The light expands and covers everything, extending to infinity forever shining and with no break or limit anywhere. Within it everything is joined in perfect continuity. Nor is it possible to imagine that anything could be outside, for there is nowhere that this light is not.

This is the vision of the Son of God, whom you know well. Here is the sight of him who knows his Father. Here is the memory of what you are; a part of this, with all of it within, and joined to all as surely as all is joined in you.[19]

PURSAH: And now we'll be silent for five minutes and join with God in a condition of perfect oneness and gratitude. We love you, Father. God Is.

NOTE: At that point I let go and tried to join with God. I felt myself expand and release the idea of borders or limits of any kind. I had no words in my mind, just the thought of a beautiful and pristine white light that extended forever. There was no friction, nothing to stop me. In fact, there was no "me." Instead of doing the thinking, it was as if I were being *thought* by God. And this thought was perfect.

Because it was perfect, it was whole, full, and complete. It was invulnerable and immortal, something that couldn't be touched by the world or threatened in any way. You cannot be attacked in perfect oneness because there's nothing else to attack you. So the feeling is one of absolute safety and fearlessness. In this condition, a state of thankfulness is very appropriate. The Song of Prayer is a song of gratitude. I felt joy by being in the presence of my Creator. I felt like saying, "Thank you, thank you," but I didn't want to bring words into this. I just wanted to have the experience.

There could be nothing missing here. There was no scarcity. There was also no possibility of death. Death represented an opposite to life, but as *A Course in Miracles* puts it: ". . . what is all-encompassing can have no opposite."[20] There was constancy, a state that does not exist in the universe of time and space, but which is the underlying experience in a state of perfect reality that is absolute stillness. The kind of extension that takes place is a simultaneous extension of the whole and is not the same as the idea of movement. Also, it was without time. I had the feeling that there was no "next," just the experience itself, and with no need for anything to follow it. It was exquisite, it was happiness, it was God.

I stayed in this experience for a while. I don't know exactly how long. I felt weightless and had no need to come back to the room I had thought I was in. Then I heard Arten speak up, and I knew it was time to try to continue our discussion.

ARTEN: *A Course in Miracles* is not a religion. It's not something you have to believe in or proselytize for. You don't have to convince anyone it's the right way. At the end of the day, spirituality is a personal thing. It's something that's done between you and the Holy Spirit or Jesus or J or Y'shua or whatever you want to call it. It doesn't matter. In the end, it leads to a personal experience of our intimate relationship with God. It's like a perfect, cosmic orgasm that can't possibly be put into words.

There aren't a lot of rules in *A Course in Miracles,* which proves it isn't a religion. But you are asked to follow instructions in the Workbook. For example, you're not supposed to do more than one Workbook lesson per day. So it should take you at least a year, if not longer, to do the Workbook.

GARY: I had a guy come up to me once and say very proudly, "I did the Workbook in six months."

ARTEN: Yes, some people can't follow even *one* rule. And there is another *unwritten* rule that should be obvious to you. The rule is this: When it comes to the *Course,* you've got to do it. If you don't do it, you can't derive the benefits of doing it. The *Course* takes a certain amount of work. That's why one of its books is called a *Workbook.* The *Course* is a spiritual discipline. It asks something of its students, and offers a lot as well. Anything worth having is worth working for, and enlightenment is more than worth having.

GARY: On the other hand, there's a paradox. Well, actually there are several paradoxes in the *Course,* but the one I'm talking about is this. I used to think it would take a tremendous amount of work to forgive the world like J did. But what I've learned more and more as I go along is that it actually takes more time to judge people than it does to forgive them! I mean, as you go along, forgiveness becomes so much a part of you that eventually you won't have to think about it as much. It will become more and more automatic. So the amount of time it takes to do it decreases over the years. But if you spend your time judging people, now you have to make up some story about why they're not worthy of your forgiveness. It would take less time to just forgive the bastards.

PURSAH: Very true, brother. And since we're talking about forgiveness, let's mention once again what kind of forgiveness we're talking about. The old-fashioned, Newtonian, subject-and-object kind of forgiveness is useless—the kind where you're forgiving people because you think they've really done something. It just keeps the idea of separation real in the unconscious mind.

True forgiveness releases people because they haven't really done anything, because you're the one who made them up in the first place. What you're seeing is *your* projection of a universe of time and space. You've taken responsibility for making it up, not in a bad way but in a powerful way. Now you're coming from cause and not effect. This is the thought reversal that the *Course* is talking about.

It also allows the Holy Spirit to heal that which is hidden in the deep canyons of your unconscious mind: the guilt you didn't know about that goes all the way back to the original idea of being separate from God, which is the so-called original sin that is really the source of your upsets. But then you assign the reason for your upset to be something outside of yourself, because that's where you projected it. So you think you're upset because you're not going to have enough money for your retirement, or because the terrorists are going to blow up your airplane, and you forget that it's not the projection at all that's *really* upsetting you, but its source in the mind. And the solution lies in your forgiveness of this illusory projection, which is your small part of the job, allowing the Holy

Spirit to take care of the big part of the job, which is the healing that you can't see but can experience.

Thus, as you forgive, there will be fundamental shifts that will be taking place in your unconscious mind, and eventually your experience will start to change. You'll gradually shift from the experience of being a body to the experience of being what you really are, which is love, or pure spirit, which in the Course are synonymous, because at the level of spirit they are exactly the same as God.

ARTEN: Perhaps it would also be helpful to remind you once again that this love is *perfect* love. It's not the world's idea of love. This love is not only perfect, but as both the Bible and *A Course in Miracles* say, *Perfect love casts out fear.* Perfect love and fear cannot coexist. Perfect love is all-encompassing. This is a kind of love that you cannot withhold from anyone or else you will not experience it for yourself. If it's not all-encompassing, then it's not real.

So there's something that's worth repeating here. If you tell people to choose love instead of fear, which is a superficial teaching unless it's explained much further, most of them will think you're talking about *their* love. But that's not what the *Course* is talking about. It's talking about the perfect love of God. The world's idea of love is what the *Course* would call *special* love, because it doesn't apply to everyone, only those special individuals whom you have chosen to love. Most people also have special hate relationships in their lives that they've chosen to project their unconscious guilt onto. And of course, it's possible to do both by having a love-hate relationship. But in the case of special love and special hate, it's obviously a lot easier to forgive the ones you think you love and very difficult to forgive the ones you don't think you love. The thing to remember is that *real* love forgives everyone and every-thing without exception. It knows what people really are. They're not real people. They're perfect love, which is the same way they were created by God.

They may think they're people. They may even think they're in-telligent. But let me tell you something, Gary. Intelligence without love is nothing. So the kind of real love we're talking about would not be people's love but the Holy Spirit's love. The Holy Spirit is the representative of God on this level. He is the memory of what you are. The Holy Spirit sees innocence everywhere because He sees everyone as being the same as Him. That's why forgiveness is the Holy Spirit's great teaching aid. It leads to the experience of perfect love. And this is the experience of being *all* of it. As the *Course* says, "God is not willing that His Son be content with less than everything."[21]

> **The thing to remember is that *real* love forgives everyone and everything without exception.**

GARY: You've explained forgiveness to me in many different ways, all of them in harmony with one another. I still see it as being three different steps that become one as you go along, because you get so used to doing it.

First, you have to stop reacting to the world, which makes it real. You have to *stop* thinking with the ego. If you catch yourself judging or condemning anything or anybody—or starting to feel a little uncomfortable, anxious, or even angry—you can be sure that's the ego. The Holy Spirit wouldn't do that. So you have to monitor your feelings as well as your thoughts. In fact, you're more likely to act out of your feelings than anything. Yet your feelings come as a result of what you think.

Once you stop thinking with the ego, you can start thinking with the Holy Spirit. You can't do both at the same time. They represent two complete and mutually exclusive thought systems. So you switch from the ego to the Holy Spirit, and that's the Holy Instant.

What would the Holy Spirit advise you to do about the situation? *Stop making it real.* Your judgments and reactions make it real, but now you can realize that the reason you see them as being guilty is because you wanted the guilt to be in them instead of you. So to undo it, you reverse the projection. You realize the guilt is *not* in them but in you, except it's not really in you either, because the whole concept of guilt was made up by the ego to make it real!

So the second part is you realize the ego made the whole thing up, and that what you're seeing is not true. There is no universe of time and space. There is only a projection of a universe of time and space. So you're not a victim of it. There's no power in being a victim, but there's plenty of power in being at cause.

Then the third thing is you change your mind about it. You choose once again, as the *Course* puts it in the last section of the Text. You overlook the body and choose to think in terms of spirit. You stop making it real and look past the veil to the truth, which is innocence everywhere, because God is everywhere. Nobody's guilty, including you. All is released to the Holy Spirit in peace. As you practice, you find that this process can be done more and more quickly, because it becomes a truth that you just know.

Plus, you're getting so used to the idea of the world coming *from* you instead of *at* you, it becomes more and more impossible for you to react to it the way you used to. Now forgiveness is justified.

PURSAH: Very nice, brother. You've been taught well. And of course you experience more as you go along that *you* are the one who's really being forgiven. As you let go of judgment and replace it with forgiveness, you can feel yourself being freed.

GARY: Yeah. It's like the Buddhist saying that judging someone is like drinking poison and then waiting for someone else to die. All judgment is really self-judgment, and all forgiveness is really self-forgiveness.

ARTEN: Amen. And since the idea is to switch from seeing things with the ego—which is the part of your mind that believes in separation, and even desires separation because it feels special—to instead seeing things with the Holy Spirit—who believes only in God and His Kingdom—then we can start to engage in a really constructive use of consciousness. Since we've learned that consciousness is really just separation, then it should be emphasized that the only truly constructive use of consciousness is to use it to choose to think with the Holy Spirit *instead* of the ego. *That* is the *Course*'s idea of free will. No matter how complicated life seems to get, no matter how many billions of people and millions of choices there seem to be, there are always really just two things to choose between, and only one of those choices represents reality. That reality is love. And love has forgotten no one. By following the Holy Spirit, you will be led to the experience of that reality.

GARY: And of course some other experiences will happen along the way. You'll feel more inspired, less like a body and more like spirit. You'll feel closer to God and other people. You may even feel like you're developing spiritual gifts as you go along, like the ability to heal others. I remember when I'd been doing the *Course* for a couple of years, my Aunt Marsha in Massachusetts called me. She had cancer, and I tried to heal her over the phone. I felt like I really made a difference, and that maybe I was getting really good as a healer.

ARTEN: She died.

GARY: You've gotta take the bad with the good. In any case, as you forgive others you're forgiven, so you get more in touch with your innocence. You feel less guilty. I think it's ironic that even though you're realizing more and more that the world isn't real, you actually end up enjoying it more, not less. I mean, when people first get into this kind of work, they think that they're giving something up by seeing it as being a dream that's not real. But what I find is that I enjoy my life *more*. It's like when I go to the movies. I know it's not real, but that doesn't stop me from enjoying it. In fact, I enjoy it more. I like listening to music more today than ever. To me, this isn't about giving up the walks on the beach or the beautiful sunsets or the great art. The less guilty you feel and the less fear you feel, the more you enjoy those things.

PURSAH: That's a good point, Gary. This is a win-win situation. You get to have a normal life. You can have your cake and eat it, too.

And the *Course* is very practical in the sense that even though you stop making the world real, you will still receive *Guidance* from the Holy Spirit as to what you should do while you appear to be here.

GARY: Yeah. I mean people come up to me sometimes on a break at a workshop; and they think they have to give up money, sex, their goals and dreams, and even their relationships. I've got news for them. Thirty or forty years from now, they'll have to do that anyway. The body isn't gonna last forever. So why not use that time to build something that *will* last forever. *That* is the difference between building your house upon the rock or upon the sand. And you know what? You can still have the sand, too! You can live your normal life, forgive as you go along, and still build your house upon the rock of God. This is a very practical spiritual path because it's not about changing your life—it's about changing your mind about your life.

PURSAH: You mean maybe J knew what he was doing?

GARY: Yeah, he did. I do have a question for you though. The language in the *Course*. Some people get upset because J always uses the word *He* in describing the Holy Spirit and God and stuff. Then there's the Shakespearean blank verse and the *Course*'s iambic pentameter, as opposed to the Koran, which is in Islamic pentameter—just kidding—and people think the language of the *Course* isn't very reader friendly. What do you think about that?

PURSAH: A couple of points. Shakespeare certainly helped Dr. Helen Schucman, the scribe of the *Course,* get through the seven years it took her to work with J and write down what she heard him say. By the way, the Foundation for Inner Peace, the original publishers of the *Course,* have put out a DVD where you can actually hear Helen describe in her own words what it was like to hear the Voice, as she called it, and work with it all those years. It was thought that Helen's voice had never been recorded, but it turned out there was an old tape-recorded interview from the late '70s that got stuck in a box for 25 years because it sounded too scratchy to be usable. But with more modern technology, it was possible to clean it up, get rid of the background noise, and make Helen's voice very understandable. It's worth listening to and seeing the slide show on the DVD because you get Helen in her own voice, which was never available before. It was recorded just three years before she made her transition. You'll be able to tell how sharp and quick she was, and how her experience was certainly genuine, not that you need proof.

But getting back to the *Course* language, Helen loved Shakespeare, and J using Shakespeare helped her. It also helped to keep the language uniform. The *Course* quotes from the King James

Version of the Bible over 800 times, often correcting or clarifying it. So the gender is male. *But,* if you truly understand what the *Course* is saying, then you realize that there is no male or female in spirit. Why? Because there are no differences or distinctions, no opposites or counterparts. There is only perfect oneness. Let the *Course* be what it is: a spiritual work of art, not a social statement. Remember what it says in the Gospel of Thomas, which is a work near and dear to our hearts: ". . . when you make male and female into a single one, so the male will not be male and the female will not be female . . . then you will enter the Kingdom."

One other point about the language. Shakespeare's writing is a classic form of language. You could go back and read things that were written in English 500 years ago in the vernacular, and you might be surprised. In many cases, words have changed so much and their spelling has changed so much that what you're reading can look like gibberish. Language is not a constant. It varies from century to century. But Shakespearean style, being a classic form of language, does not vary from century to century. Thus, people can read it and understand it, even if it's not always easy.

GARY: I get what you're saying. Even if it's not always easy, people will still be able to understand the *Course* 500 years from now or even a thousand years from now, because it's written in a classic form instead of the vernacular. It won't be dated, because it is timeless. I never thought of that. It's brilliant. Hey, maybe the J guy does have something on the ball—I mean, aside from being perfect and forgiving the world and stuff.

ARTEN: You can forgive the world, too, Gary. All you have to do is forgive whatever comes up in front of your face on any given day. The relationships you seem to be in, the situations you seem to be stuck in, the awful events you sometimes see on television or maybe even in person, the bad memories that come into your mind—all can be forgiven. They're all the same. You can forgive other bodies, or you can forgive your own body. They're the same, too. You can release the resentment that you have toward others or the regrets that you have about your own life. You just do it one day at a time, and then the day will come when your job will be done.

PURSAH: We're going to take our leave, but we'll be coming to see you when we know it will be helpful. We always have our reasons as to when we appear.

At this time of Christmas, allow me to quote from the *Course* that you love, and let us join with the Holy Spirit in peace. Many people misunderstood J's message 2,000 years ago. Because of the manner of his death, they assumed his message was one of suffering and sacrifice. They also believed this because their previous religion had a long tradition of sacrifice. But nothing could be further from J's real message. The following quote is from the section in the Text of the *Course* called "Christmas as the End of Sacrifice." When we leave, remember that to experience real love, you must learn that even though the most special relationships will demand some form of sacrifice, love wants only that there be love.

Love wants only that there be love.

> This Christmas give the Holy Spirit everything that would hurt you. Let yourself be healed completely that you may join with Him in healing, and let us celebrate our release together by releasing everyone with us. Leave nothing behind, for release is total, and when you have accepted it with me you will give it with me. All pain and sacrifice and littleness will disappear in our relationship, which is as innocent as our relationship with our Father, and as powerful. Pain will be brought to us and disappear in our presence, and without pain there can be no sacrifice. And without sacrifice there love *must* be.[22]

2

A TOUR OF THE IN-BETWEEN LIFE

This year is thus the time to make the easiest decision that ever confronted you, and also the only one. You will cross the bridge into reality simply because you will recognize that God is on the other side, and nothing at all is here. It is impossible not to make the natural decision as this is realized.[1]

On January 22, 2007, Arten and Pursah paid me their second visit of the series. I'd just conducted my first workshop of the year at the Kripalu Yoga Center in Western Massachusetts. My hand had improved dramatically in the three and a half weeks between Arten and Pursah's first appearance of the series and that weekend workshop at Kripalu. I had no trouble signing books, carrying my luggage, or shaking hands with the participants. I was enormously relieved. Although I had great confidence by now in the forgiveness process and the fact that it could be applied to anything, it was still fun to see it work in my life. I was also excited because my teachers had said they'd talk even more about that process, and how it applies to healing the body, during one of our discussions in this series.

I knew I was about to lead a workshop in Miami and, in the following weeks, the islands of Kauai and Oahu in Hawaii. I was looking forward to visiting such exotic locations, especially in the middle of the winter. I was no fan of cold weather, ice, or snow; and anytime I could escape Maine at that time of year was a welcomed opportunity. I didn't know this would be the last winter I'd ever live in a cold climate.

My wife, Karen, had studied *A Course in Miracles* for about two years a decade ago. She did this mainly because of my interest in it. She even came to the same study group as me for a couple of years. Then she gave up on it. After that, the two of us started to grow in different directions. She developed her own interests, including starting her own business. My life became more about the *Course,* eventually leading me to travel a great deal to teach it. That drove even more of a wedge between us, because I wasn't home as long as she wanted me to be, and she was forced to spend a lot of time alone. I didn't feel we were ready yet financially for her to quit her job and travel with me. It was a divisive dilemma for both of us.

When Arten and Pursah showed up for this particular visit, they seemed a little more serious than usual. Pursah began the discussion.

PURSAH: We have a lot to cover today, brother. First, your hand is better. Congratulations on applying the teachings. You're getting the universal implications of the kind of forgiveness we've been teaching you. Also, you've got an eventful month coming up. We want to help prepare you for it. But first, we have a surprise for you.

GARY: A good surprise, I hope?

PURSAH: Yes, it is. We've pointed out in the past that the *Course* says the direction of the mind is automatic, depending on the thought system to which it adheres.[2] If you're thinking right-minded, or forgiveness thoughts, with the Holy Spirit, you have to be headed in the right direction. That direction is home to God. If you're thinking judgmental and condemning thoughts with the ego, then you keep yourself away from God.

ARTEN: Most people who are into spirituality assume that when the body passes away and they go to the so-called afterlife, they then make decisions and contracts and commitments as to how and what they're going to do in their next incarnation. No! Those incarnations are already over. What they do is reexperience a movie that's already been filmed. Now, what people call the afterlife is actually an in-between life. It's the period spent between one dream lifetime, the details of which had already been determined, and the next dream lifetime, the details of which have already been determined. The freedom, or free will, that exists for them during those dream lifetimes is the ability to choose the Holy Spirit's interpretation of everything instead of the ego's. Whether or not they do that and achieve real healing will determine the nature of their in-between lifetime experience, as well as which lifetime they will experience after that!

That's why it's so important that you don't wait to practice forgiveness. Don't wait until next year. Don't wait until your next lifetime. Your future is being determined by you right *now*, depending on the choices you make: on whether you choose the Holy Spirit's interpretation of what you're seeing or the ego's.

Your next dream lifetime, if you review another lifetime, may not be in the same order as the seeming linear sequence. The next lifetime you experience could be one that appeared to happen 500 years ago, or a thousand years ago, or a hundred years from now. It doesn't matter. The nature of that lifetime and which forgiveness lessons it holds will depend on whether or not you learn the forgiveness opportunities that are presented to you *now*. That's why it's crucial to take advantage of the lessons that are presented to you on any given day. Those are the lessons the Holy Spirit wants you to learn. If you learn them—and you do so by practicing true forgiveness, the kind that comes from cause and not effect—then you won't have to repeat the same kinds of patterns all over again in your next dream lifetime. You get to move on to a place where you'll be able to make additional progress, and perhaps even complete *all* of your forgiveness lessons and go home. Of course, it's possible for you to do that in this lifetime, depending on how committed you are and whether or not you forgive everything that comes up.

As the *Course* puts it, and this applies to this lifetime or any lifetime, "Trials are but lessons that you failed to learn presented once again, so where you made a faulty choice before you now can make a better one, and thus escape all pain that what you chose before has brought to you."[3]

> You get to move on to a place where you'll be able to make additional progress.

GARY: So let's say you fail to learn a forgiveness lesson that's presented to you. That quote says the lessons will be presented once again, but I take it that the lesson won't necessarily be presented in exactly the same form. It could be a similar event, situation, or relationship that gives you an equivalent challenge.

ARTEN: That's right. Obviously, a lesson that's presented a hundred years from now won't look *exactly* the same as a lesson does today. It's the meaning and content that stay the same, even though the form may appear to change.

PURSAH: So, we said we have a surprise for you. The three of us are going on a little trip. But first, let's point out that there are many different kinds of mind travel. The humans of Earth believe in a rudimentary form of travel at the level of the physical that's powered by forms of matter. They never stop to think how primitive it is. At times we've given you examples of a much more advanced form of travel, which we call mind transport. This is *not* the same as remote viewing, where you seem to stay in one place physically but view things at distances, sometimes great distances. Obviously, it's also *not* astral travel, where a lighter, energy-based body appears to go with you. With mind transport you seem to take your physical body with you and experience everything the senses have to offer. It seems as completely real as anything you experience when you appear to be in a physical body.

I wanted to explain that because it's not just a form of traveling you can do here; it's also the form of travel that most aliens use to visit Earth. If you wanted to visit a place that was 50 billion light-years away, then even if you traveled at the speed of light it would take you 50 billion years to get there. Hardly practical.

However, once you master the art of mind transport, it takes you *no* time to travel those 50 billion light-years.

GARY: So that would explain the seemingly impossible speeds and maneuvers that UFOs make. The aliens are using the mind to travel, and they're not dependent on physical laws. In fact, they transcend physical laws.

PURSAH: Yes, and the *Course* says that's possible, but puts it in the perspective of holiness: "Your holiness reverses all the laws of the world. It is beyond every restriction of time, space, distance and limits of any kind."[4] Now the kind of travel we're going to use for this excursion is astral travel. That's because it's the most common type of travel that people experience during the in-between life. Many people think of the astral body as being the soul, but they don't know that the concept of having an individual soul is a separation idea, while real spirit is whole, undivided, and has no personal identity.

We're going to give you a brief tour of the kinds of things you may see during your in-between life. As both the Buddhists and the *Course* say, ". . . birth was not the beginning, and death is not an end."[5] The closer you are to your final lifetime, the more the in-between life will look like the present-day universe. If you're not that spiritually advanced, then you'll see all kinds of wild things, as in that movie you liked, *What Dreams May Come.*

A few days after J raised Lazarus from the dead, some Roman soldiers caught up with Lazarus with orders to kill him. Pilate didn't want any formerly dead people walking around. The soldiers asked Lazarus, "What's it like on the other side?" And Lazarus replied, "It's like this." He was very spiritually advanced. Then the soldiers killed him—he died twice that time around.

The in-between life can show you many different kinds of images, and it's not our intention to make any of this real. But it will sure *seem* real. Are you ready?

GARY: Ah, no?

NOTE: At that point I felt as if I were leaving my body. It was amazing, as though there was suddenly no physical encumbrance. I still seemed to be contained within a space that had limits like a body, but there was no physical sensation. There was, however, a sort of mental sensation. I could sense that Arten and Pursah were with me, but I couldn't see them. Then suddenly I heard Arten speak by way of mental telepathy.

ARTEN: Right now it seems to you that you're still within a certain limited space. That's the thought of separation again. Whether it's time, space, bodies, astral bodies, or whatever, it's all based on the idea of separation. Obviously, there's no physical pain in the state you're in. That can be very exhilarating, especially at first. However, there's still the possibility of psychological pain, which we'll get to.

GARY: I can't wait. Hey, I can communicate, but it feels strange. I'm not talking. There are no lips! And I'm not breathing! This is wild.

ARTEN: The belief that you have to breathe when you're in a human body is just that: a belief. That's also true with death itself—it's just a belief. Everything is in the mind. In fact, you still experience, even after you appear to leave your physical body, that you're seeing what you're seeing with your eyes. But you're not. You're "seeing" with the mind. The body, whether it be human, astral, or otherwise, isn't really there because it's just as much a part of the projection as the rest of the projection. As J tells us in the Course, "At no single instant does the body exist at all."[6] As we go along here, your astral body may seem to disappear and you'll sense that you're viewing everything with the mind, but that's a very advanced state.

NOTE: I then experienced myself rising higher and higher. I could start to see the curvature of the Earth. There was no hot or cold, only a very light and ephemeral floating. I seemed to be more and more connected to the space around me, as though I was joining with it. I could see different continents, some partially covered with clouds, and then I shot up into outer space, leaving the color of the Earth's sky and heading into darkness, although I could still see the blue planet I thought was my home.

Suddenly I seemed to be racing, going faster and faster. I flew past the moon and toward Mars—a planet which Arten and Pursah once told me had life in the past, life that eventually migrated to Earth. As I viewed the planet, the mental feeling was awesome. Then I quickly passed and viewed several other recognizable planets before catapulting out of the solar system.

Then things really started to seem strange! I felt my mind was the power behind the movement, not the astral body, and that was fun. But some of the things I saw were unfamiliar to me. As I went farther and farther out into the universe at what seemed to be an unbelievable speed, there was an unexpected feeling of conflict. Then I saw what appeared to be two galaxies, but they seemed to be at odds with each other.

ARTEN: Here you see an example of the thought of conflict within being given form in a place that seems to be without. When the *Course* says that what you're seeing is the outside picture of an inward condition[7], it means it literally. There's a black hole in one of the galaxies, and it's shooting a stream of radiation and energy at the other galaxy.

GARY: Are you saying these galaxies are at war? You're kidding!

ARTEN: Not at all. One galaxy passes another, and the other attacks it. Violent radiation particles are being hurled from one to the other. It may be hard for you to believe, but separation is played out everywhere in the projection of time and space.

GARY: So it's not just people.

PURSAH: Correct. And now, you're going to see something *really* different. Remember, in a dream it's possible to show you anything you want and for you to project anything you want. It's just a question of removing the barriers that prevent you from having complete access to the power of the mind.

NOTE: In the distance I saw what appeared to be a spaceship of some kind. It kept getting bigger and bigger. Then it started to become mammoth, giving me a sense of awe. I spoke to Arten again, although I couldn't see him.

GARY: What the hell is that?

ARTEN: It's a Pleiadian starship. It's on a simple mission to patrol its own galaxy. But it's very possible for it to go anywhere—including the Earth—instantly.

GARY: I thought that race of beings was from the past.

ARTEN: No. They're still in business. Nice group. Very advanced. And as more of them become enlightened, there are fewer and fewer of them who appear to be here. We've said the mind keeps dividing and showing up here as images. But when a race like the Pleiadians starts to become enlightened, more of them start leaving the hologram and going home to God. So the enlightened being does not come back, and the population starts to go down. You eventually have more beings getting enlightened and leaving the illusion than being born. Then the race will disappear, but in a good way, home to God, not in a bad way. Do you want to go on board?

GARY: Now you're screwing with me.

PURSAH: Let's go, cowboy.

NOTE: A second later I found myself on a spaceship in an area that was so huge it seemed impossible. How could anyone make something of this size? Then two beings came out of nowhere and dropped down in front of me. They looked human, but bigger, and both had blond hair.

PURSAH: Pleiadians can look human to you, but more attractive, even to humans. This is their Nordic look. They also have an alternate appearance that they haven't chosen to show you.

GARY: Why not? I can handle it.

PURSAH: We can't interfere with a race's decisions.

GARY: Oh, I get it. The prime directive, right?

PURSAH: Something like that. Do you want to ask these beings a question?

There were two men, and I asked them, "How do you control a ship so vast?"

One of them answered, "The same way it was built: by the mind. We can go anywhere we want without having to traverse space. We are there in the blink of an eye. The human race will be able to do that eventually, but you've got quite a ways to go."

"Incidentally," the being continued, "it's possible for a human to live his or her next lifetime as a member of an alien race, even a Pleiadian."

"Awesome!" But before I could go on, the being said, "That's determined by the way you think. We'd like to talk with you some more, but we sense you should finish your little trip. Be well."

Then we appeared to be outside the gigantic ship and took off at another high rate of movement and passed what a Voice in my mind told me was Sirius, and then Orion. My mind was starting to spin as we slowed down and stopped.

PURSAH: Look over there. What do you see?

GARY: I'm not sure. It looks like a tunnel of sorts.

PURSAH: It's a wormhole. A lot of your scientists believe they hold the best possibility of traveling from one part of the universe to another, and they can sometimes be used that way. You can even travel through time. That's the way most races do it at first, but mind transport is still the best way to go.

GARY: Hey, if I'm in the so-called in-between life, then why am I seeing so many things that appear to be in real time?

PURSAH: Simple, Gary. That's because *none* of it is real! So during the in-between phase, people will see what they're ready to see. That can vary widely.

We then accelerated back in the general direction I felt we had come from. I intuited that we were heading toward Earth, but on the way were things I didn't understand.

PURSAH: There you see matter being destroyed by antimatter. It comes from stars being ripped apart by neutron stars and black holes.

GARY: I didn't realize the universe outside of our own solar system was so violent.

The universe is not really based on the idea of unity.

PURSAH: The universe is not really based on the idea of unity. The only reason it even holds together is because, being all part of the same projection, there is only one projection. Thus, you can't ever *really* break it apart. Yet it will appear to be falling apart and dividing and subdividing many times.

As we continued, I saw a sun, which I assumed was our own. I could see lines of magnetic fields and what looked like waves running along them.

ARTEN: Those are solar ripples. They carry your sun's energy in all different directions. They're an important component of the electromagnetic system that regulates the movement of your solar system, along with gravity, and as they move out across the universe, they're connected to similar actions everywhere.

As I raced toward the sun I could see the planets of my solar system again, and the Earth was fast approaching. We reentered the atmosphere and moved in the direction of North America. We zoomed in on a particular part of the country that I knew wasn't the area that I lived in. A city got closer and closer and, having been to Chicago, I recognized its position on Lake Michigan. There was a larger skyline than I remembered, and as we zoomed in there were individual buildings, and then one that looked like a hospital, because it had what appeared to be an emergency entrance. Yet the buildings were different from what I was used to. They were more futuristic.

Then all of a sudden, I was inside what looked like an operating room. I could see that a woman was about to give birth.

GARY: Who's that?

PURSAH: That's our mother.

GARY: *What?!*

PURSAH: She is our mother, and I'm about to be born in your next lifetime. When you've completed your in-between life, you'll be automatically guided to this place and time in the hologram, where you'll appear to be born as me.

GARY: *Now* it's getting weird. You're saying that's me in that woman's tummy, and this is the beginning of our final lifetime?

PURSAH: Yes. We wanted to show you how you end up starting over again, with another chance to learn the lessons that you haven't. Now in your case, those lessons will be few. You may not have always been the smoothest practitioner of forgiveness when you were Gary, but your quality of perseverance paid off.

Let's go to a higher realm, which you've earned. You earned it by practicing true forgiveness, from cause and not effect, and the result was real healing by the Holy Spirit. The awareness you're about to experience will show you the quality of the in-between life you're going to have before the lifetime that you appear to re-incarnate as Pursah. We skipped this part, which would have come *first* in your between-life experience, because we wanted to show it to you independently. But when you replay your in-between life upon the setting aside of Gary's body, you'll first encounter what we're about to show you. Then after that, and everything else you just saw, you'll appear to go inside that little baby's body, although you're never really inside of a body. Come with us, brother.

NOTE: We were then in an entirely different kind of place. There was a beautiful whitish glow around me. This light felt warm and healing; tingly, inviting, and orgasmic. I felt a bliss that has only come to me in revelation—those few times when I felt I had truly joined with God.

I then remembered a wonderful passage from the part of *A Course in Miracles* called The Song of Prayer, for it captured what I was feeling. I hadn't memorized the *Course* verbatim, but there were many parts of it that stood out so much for me that I could easily recall them and speak them by heart. This was one of them, and I thought of the beautiful words in my mind. Then I became silent. I knew Arten and Pursah were there with me, but it also felt like everyone was there with me. I felt gratitude that it was possible to actually experience what The Song of Prayer said:

> This is what death should be; a quiet choice, made joyfully and with a sense of peace, because the body has been kindly used to help the Son of God along the way he goes to God. We thank the body, then, for all the service it has given us. But we are thankful, too, the need is done to walk the world of limits, and to reach the Christ in hidden forms and clearly seen at most in lovely flashes. Now we can behold Him without blinders, in the light that we have learned to look upon again.
>
> We call it death, but it is liberty. It does not come in forms that seem to be thrust down in pain upon unwilling flesh, but as a gentle welcome to release. If there has been true healing, this can be the form in which death comes when it is time to rest a while from labor gladly done and gladly ended. Now we go in peace to freer air and gentler climate, where it is not hard to see the gifts we gave were saved for us. For Christ is clearer now; His vision more sustained in us; His Voice, the Word of God, more certainly our own.[8]

This condition seemed to last for a while, but I didn't know how long. Within it I temporarily stopped thinking. There was no body, and the mind was invisible. If I stayed this way forever, I wouldn't have complained, but eventually I started to feel uncomfortable. What was this? It was as though I felt like there was something wrong—even as if I had done something wrong. I didn't understand, but I knew it was a feeling I'd like to get away from. Then suddenly I was back at my place, sitting in front of my two ascended visitors. I was almost too dumbstruck to speak, yet bursting with questions.

GARY: That was incredible! I never knew I could feel that free, although the trip you showed me most of the way wasn't as good as the feeling I had at the end of being one with my Source. But there are a couple of things I don't understand. Like, I hear all these stories people tell about the afterlife, and they seem different and very detailed—for example, seeing all kinds of crystal castles and amazing scenes with beautiful visions that include them creating things with their thoughts and all that stuff. How does that fit in?

PURSAH: That's why we said earlier that people will see what they're ready to see.

ARTEN: A person can only see what he or she is prepared for. And when we say *see,* we always mean with the mind. *See* actually means the way you think. Once again, spiritual sight is done at the level of the mind, and has absolutely nothing to do with what the body appears to see. The body can't see or do anything anyway! But the mind can always choose to use it in the service of the Holy Spirit instead of the ego.

Spiritual sight is done at the level of the mind.

GARY: Okay, so let's assume for a minute that I'm not completely out of it and everything I just saw was a part of the universe of time and space that we all appear to share. You're saying that people's in-between life experience will vary widely, depending on what they believe and what they're ready to experience?

PURSAH: Of course. You were practicing forgiveness and will continue to do so in this illusory lifetime. That will result in a good experience for you when you appear to make your transition. What just appeared to happen was an excellent experience compared to what some people will go through. People often start off as seeing what they expect to, from long-lost relatives to beautiful colors that are almost beyond description, to a long tunnel and what looks like the light. They'll even have beautiful visions that leave them amazed by the so-called wonder of the universe that's beyond what they'd call life in the body.

But it doesn't last, and then they experience the uncomfortableness that you started to feel, except it's often a lot worse. It's a psychological pain that they want to get away from. It's a replay of the original time of the seeming separation from their Source and the guilt they felt as a result of it. So they run away from it by hiding in a body and end up in the position you just appeared to be in at that hospital: a helpless little victim, a baby that they assume could not possibly be responsible for *anything.* But of course the truth is that you're responsible for *everything* and then you forget it.

That's why we stress how important it is for you to take advantage of your forgiveness opportunities *now*. The more you learn through application, the better your future experiences will be, whether or not you appear to be on Earth.

GARY: So I have to forgive all the little things as well as the big things. I need to get that there's not really anybody out there who's selling more books than I am, and there's not really anybody for me to use my mind to try to meet. You know, like using the Law of Attraction except on a person.

ARTEN: Well, for the last two years, you *have* been focusing on Shakira.

GARY: Hey, some call it stalking, I call it love.

PURSAH: The Law of Attraction doesn't work for most people anyway, which we'll get into a little later. Incidentally, if people want to see a better version of The Law of Attraction and The Secret, they could read Napoleon Hill's classic book, *Think and Grow Rich*. It was first published back in the 1930s. Today, people will say things like, "da Vinci used The Secret, and Edison used The Secret," except they leave out one of the most important parts. Those guys worked their butts off! And even then, there's a more important part that people don't teach because they don't know about it. We'll get to it later.

ARTEN: It's been said that success is 10 percent inspiration and 90 percent perspiration. Many times that's true. For example, you have a reputation of being kind of a slacker, mainly because of things the three of us said in your first book. But the truth is that you've worked very hard the last few years. Sometimes that's what it takes. You have a higher degree of difficulty than most spiritual teachers, because you're not just telling your listeners what they want to hear. Considering what the *Course* is teaching, and what you're saying at your workshops, you and your books and CDs are doing very well, even better than could be expected. But you had to work extremely hard in order to help make that happen.

GARY: Then the rest is up to the Holy Spirit.

PURSAH: Exactly, and it works. *But,* it may be wise for you to slow down at least a *little.* Why don't you take off at least one weekend every month? That way you'd be home 10 or 11 days in a row each month. It would give you more time to write, yet you'd still be traveling more than enough to spread the message.

GARY: I guess I could do that. Maybe next year—I'm already booked for this year. So you really think I should make more time for myself?

PURSAH: Yes, and there's another reason. You've done two books, which is fine, but we want you to start doing more books. People can't hear this kind of a teaching often enough, and you not only help to reinforce the *Course* for people, but you also introduce new students to it.

GARY: I may need more than one weekend off a month if I'm gonna do more books.

ARTEN: All right. Enough career counseling. How would you say your marriage is going?

GARY: Well, it's been difficult, and it's not like we haven't tried. We've been married a long time. We just can't seem to make it work, but we've had our good times, too. I think when I started traveling a lot a few years ago, it was the straw that broke the camel's back. I don't see it lasting now. We're just not on the same wavelength. Karen's a good person, always has been, but we've been going in different directions.

Say, I had to renew my driver's license recently. Why don't they make marriage licenses like driver's licenses? They could be good for five years, or whatever. Then if either spouse doesn't want to renew the license when it expires, that would be it!

ARTEN: Thank you, Gary. I'm sure I speak for Pursah and myself, as well as the entire spiritual community, when I say that we're refreshed and challenged by your unique point of view.

PURSAH: Do you have anything sane to say?

GARY: Seriously, I don't know what to do.

PURSAH: In the next month especially, but also after that, you're going to find yourself challenged on many different fronts. We've always said we wouldn't tell you too much so you can have your experiences and then forgive them, but you're going to feel overwhelmed.

GARY: Again?

PURSAH: Yes. But remember that we are with you always, watching everything. So is J. As manifestations of the Holy Spirit and Teachers of teachers, there's no one of whom we are unaware.[9]

GARY: Thank you. That means a lot to me.

ARTEN: Between now and our next visit, try to come from a place of not needing anything. If you need something, you're coming from a place of scarcity. For example, if you want some money to do something, like a project, then think of the money as being a tool you can use to extend love. It doesn't matter that you're extending it into an illusion. What matters is the love, which *is* real, and the sense of abundance that comes from needing nothing. Then you can also extend that abundance. As the *Course* puts it: "Give, therefore, of your abundance, and teach your brothers theirs."[10]

GARY: Then that would also be true with relationships. You shouldn't be going after a person because you need him or her. If you need someone, you're deprived. But if you don't need the individual, then you can join with that person out of a mutual awareness of abundance.

PURSAH: Yes. It applies to relationships, money, anything. What matters is that you're doing things with the love of the Holy Spirit, and not for the glorification of the ego. It's not what you do, it's who you are doing it with. Is it the ego or the Holy Spirit?

ARTEN: A lot of people think it's *what* they do that matters, and they use it as a subtle way of glorifying themselves and their intelligence. Yet it's really the love that matters. If you're coming from a place of love, then what you're doing can be guided by spirit.

GARY: Yeah. It's like when they discovered how to split atoms and develop something nuclear. What's the first thing they did with it? They built a bomb! That may have taken intelligence, but it certainly didn't require love.

ARTEN: That's why Einstein asked a serious question: Is the human race good?

GARY: Given the nature of the ego, that's a legitimate question. Under the dominance of the ego, the human race is at best split between good and bad, and that's on a good day. It's only if the mind is dominated by the thoughts of the Holy Spirit, which is something we have to choose for ourselves, that humans become increasingly good and eventually return to the Divine.

ARTEN: Well said.

GARY: I like what you've said about how intelligence without love is nothing.

ARTEN: You've been to *A Course in Miracles* meetings where, a lot of the time, you'll have someone in the meeting who is a know-it-all about the *Course* and has to be right about everything, and there's no room for disagreement. In your travels, you've also met many people whom the world would refer to as being mentally challenged. Isn't it interesting that a lot of these men and women seem to go through life seeing other people with love? Now, as I've told you in the past, if it's true that as you see him you will see yourself, it would also have to mean that the mentally challenged person who's going through life seeing other people with love is making more spiritual progress in this lifetime than the intellectual who would rather be right than happy!

PURSAH: How you use your mind is up to you. As Erich Fromm said, love is the answer to the problem of human existence; it's also the way home. Of course what most quickly facilitates the *experience* of love is true forgiveness, which is why we always come back to that. But remember the word *love* in the *Course* is a term that's representative of a complete thought system—the thought system of the Holy Spirit. And the word *fear* in the *Course* is also representative of a complete thought system—the thought system of the ego. The two thought systems are mutually exclusive and can *never* be reconciled. You have to choose one or the other or else your mind will be split. There are no opposites in Heaven, and in order to reenter the Kingdom of Heaven, there must be no allegiance to opposites in your mind.

There are no opposites in Heaven.

GARY: As I've allowed the Holy Spirit to take over more and more of my mind, which isn't a scary thing because the Holy Spirit is actually what I am in reality *anyway,* I've also gotten the impression that I really don't have to be concerned about the kinds of things I used to be concerned about. For example, I've noticed the last couple of years that I'm just not as interested in politics as I used to be. I think I've forgiven politicians on the TV screen so much that these things just don't have as big an effect on me as they used to.

PURSAH: Excellent. And that doesn't mean you can't vote if you want to or pay a little bit of attention. It means that you're not in a reactionary state about it, and thus much more peaceful.

GARY: Yeah, and I don't seem to be as concerned about having enough money to retire or do things. It's like I know my needs are being taken care of, and they always will be.

PURSAH: Very good. As the Psychotherapy section of the *Course* teaches you—and by the way, that section uses the word *therapist* a lot, but you could substitute that word with *healer* or *teacher* or whatever your job is, and it would mean exactly the same thing—"Even an advanced therapist has some earthly needs while he is here. Should he need money it will be given him, not in payment, but to help him better serve the plan. Money is not evil. It is nothing. But no one here can live with no illusions, for he must yet strive to have the last illusion be accepted by everyone everywhere. He has a mighty part in this one purpose, for which he came. He stays here but for this. And while he stays he will be given what he needs to stay."[11]

GARY: That's great! And it doesn't matter how it comes—it will just come if it's supposed to. Some people think it's important how it comes. I have a friend who says, "I got *my* money the old-fashioned way."

ARTEN: Ah, inheritance.

PURSAH: By the way, that quote said, "He stays here but for this." The *Course* uses the word *but* in this way because, as we discussed, it's written in Shakespearean language. But for someone like you who isn't really into Shakespeare, you could substitute the word *only* for *but* all the way through the *Course,* and it would read more smoothly in your mind.

GARY: Cool. I like little tips like that. Any more?

PURSAH: Yes, but it's not little. Remember what everything is for, no matter what happens in the next month. That's one of the things that makes this teaching so consistent and important: You always know what everything is for. It's to use for forgiveness. Instead of giving truth to your illusions, you can give your illusions to the truth.[12] The *Course* is very clear in its explanations of this. For example:

> The world is an illusion. Those who choose to come to it are seeking for a place where they can be illusions, and avoid their own reality. Yet when they find their own reality is even here, then they step back and let it lead the way. What other choice is really theirs to make?[13]

GARY: When it says, "Those who choose to come to it," I thought you said the direction of the mind was automatic depending on whether you apply forgiveness. That quote seems to be saying we make a decision to come here between lifetimes.

PURSAH: No, it's a metaphor, as is much of the *Course.* You chose to come here the original instant that you chose the ego instead of the Holy Spirit and the universe of time and space was made. From that instant on, you choose to stay here by *not* practicing forgiveness, and you choose to go home by *not* accepting the ego's interpretation of relationships, situations, and events. The reason the quote we're talking about is a metaphor is because time is holographic, yet the choices you make here *appear* to be linear. That's the paradox of time. In terms of the hologram, it has already happened, but in your linear experience, you've still got to do it.

What you want to do is refuse to take the linear nature of time seriously and make the only real choice you can make, which is simple. That choice overlooks the mad illusion of time. As the *Course* says on that same page:

> This is the simple choice we make today. The mad illusion will remain awhile in evidence, for those to look upon who chose to come, and

have not yet rejoiced to find they were mistaken in their choice. They cannot learn directly from the truth, because they have denied that it is so. And so they need a Teacher Who perceives their madness, but Who still can look beyond illusion to the simple truth in them.

If truth demanded they give up the world, it would appear to them as if it asked the sacrifice of something that is real. Many have chosen to renounce the world while still believing its reality. And they have suffered from a sense of loss, and have not been released accordingly. Others have chosen nothing but the world, and they have suffered from a sense of loss still deeper, which they did not understand.

Between these paths there is another road that leads away from loss of every kind, for sacrifice and deprivation both are quickly left behind. This is the way appointed for you now.[14]

PURSAH: And so your path is to not be *attached* to the world. It's all right that you live your life. You simply believe less and less in its reality as you continue to make the choice for holiness. By holding the reality of wholeness in the back of your mind while you go about your worldly functions, the experience of the reality of the false world is gradually undone. And as it's undone, it's naturally replaced with the experience of your true nature, which is eternal.

ARTEN: We're pleased with you, brother. Don't hesitate to call on us in your mind when you feel challenged, and we'll talk with you. We'll also see you again when the time is right.

GARY: I'm grateful to both of you, and thanks for the trip!

PURSAH: Our pleasure. You're about to take another one. Enjoy the illusion of Miami.

NOTE: Arten and Pursah disappeared simultaneously and instantaneously, as usual. Later that week I made a trip to Miami to do a workshop at the Unity on the Bay Church. Most of the congregation and workshop participants spoke Spanish, and I was going to use an interpreter for only the second time. There are two kinds of verbal translations: consecutive and simultaneous. Consecutive is where you speak a sentence or two and then you stop as the translator repeats what you just said. That's the way it's usually done if there's no equipment available for a simultaneous translation. In a consecutive translation, while you're paused and waiting for the translator, you have to remember what you just said and pick it up from there. That's not as much fun as just losing yourself in the Holy Spirit.

With a simultaneous translation, the translator speaks over a microphone that's not audible to the entire group, but the translation goes out to those wearing earphones who have elected to hear the translation. In this kind of a translation, the translator tries to keep up with you. Most speakers find it much easier to do this kind of speaking because they don't have to alter their style. They can be themselves, but they'll generally go a little slower than usual and try to help the translator. After all, it takes more words to say something in Spanish, Italian, French, and many other languages than it does in English.

I was going to get to do a simultaneous translation in Miami. My translator's name was Jesus (pronounced "Hey-suse"). Jesus was a smart and kind man. He did a great job of translating what I said, and the workshop went very well. I'd later use translators for a simultaneous translation in Mexico and have a similar result. My first book was available in Spanish, and the translators told me the translation was very good. That made me happy because I knew that *A Course in Miracles* was growing faster in Spanish than in any other language.

After the workshop, Jesus volunteered to give me a tour of the city. To me, Miami was South Beach and the city skyline, which I sometimes saw on TV. But Jesus was about to change that false impression. Several of the workshop participants decided to come along. We'd go along with Jesus as he explained the different sights we were seeing, and we'd occasionally joke that we were "following Jesus."

Shortly before I went to Miami, a bigoted American politician had visited there and said it was like a "third-world country." From what I was seeing now, that remark could only have come as a result of racism. In fact, I'd later see a survey that rated Miami as the cleanest city in America. If you want to see a third-world country in America, you'd be better off going to LaGuardia or Kennedy airports in New York. I'm sure that many first-time visitors to the U.S. are shocked by what they see. I say that because of the condition of the outdated airports. Miami, on the other hand, looked wonderful.

Jesus had a great voice and spoke his language beautifully. Spanish to me sounded almost like music. It was much more colorful and interesting than English. I've never had much of a talent for languages. It's just not a gift of mine is this lifetime. But I completely enjoyed listening to Jesus talk to his friends in Spanish. He'd then say the same thing to me in English, so I'd know what I was seeing during his generous tour.

Jesus took us through the city and drove by some of the beaches and islands I'd seen before. Then it was on to places I hadn't seen. We went through beautiful neighborhoods like Coral Gables and Coconut Grove. The palm trees, occasional waterways, well-kept landscapes, and lovely houses made the areas very attractive. And then it was on to Little Havana. We visited a Cuban cigar store, where it was rumored you could find illegal Cuban cigars in the back. We also stopped at a popular Cuban restaurant, and Jesus offered me a drink called a mojito. It was sweet, but it didn't take me long to find out it was *very* strong. Fortunately, I was smart enough to remember that I was speaking again the next day and decided not to have a second one.

I found the friendliness and warmth of my new Spanish friends to be very gratifying. And I knew that Miami was a place I wouldn't mind visiting again. Besides, I'd made good friends with a guy named Gene Bogart and his wife, Helen, who lived just 40 minutes north of there in Boca Raton, next to Fort Lauderdale. In fact, Gene had asked me to do a podcast with him. To show how technically advanced I am, I didn't even know what a podcast was. But in October of the previous year, we'd launched the *Gary Renard Podcast,* with Gene as my cohost and producer. I was surprised by the number of people all over the world who responded favorably, and we were soon in the top ten in the spiritual category at iTunes.

Gene and I had led parallel lives. We were the same age and had been professional guitar players for 20 years. We both understood *A Course in Miracles,* mainly because of my teachers and

Disappearance, and we thought the same way about many different subjects. I could now see that the Miami–Fort Lauderdale area would hold a lot of appeal for me in the future, especially when it was "in season," as Frank Sinatra used to say at the Fontainebleau Hotel. And then it hit me. I remembered what the *Course* and my teachers had asked me more than once: "What is it for?"

A Course in Miracles doesn't generally focus on forgiving the good stuff. That's not where your unconscious guilt lies and comes to the surface. The *Course* focuses especially on those times when you feel anger, or even annoyance. In fact, it teaches that anything that's an uncomfortable feeling is the same as any other uncomfortable feeling, no matter how seemingly big or small, because it's *not* peace.

> **An uncomfortable feeling is the same as any other uncomfortable feeling.**

The beauty I saw in the world, which I knew was subjective, didn't deprive me of peace. So I realized it wasn't a problem. I knew J would never want me to feel guilty, and the *Course* didn't seem very concerned about forgiving beautiful sunsets or works of art, which the *Course* itself certainly was. So I decided to remember more often that the beauty I was seeing outside of me was simply symbolic of the beauty and abundance that was within. It wasn't real, so there was no reason to be guilty about enjoying it. In fact, it was possible that "what it was for" was to make me realize that I'm not guilty, especially if I was coming from a place of love while I was enjoying things.

As for the things of this world that were obviously not beautiful, they'd keep me more than busy enough applying forgiveness.

The following week, Karen and I were off to Hawaii. I was going to lead two workshops: one on the stunning island of Kauai, and another the following week on beautiful Oahu, known as "The Gathering Place." We were also going to use the opportunity to take most of our two weeks there as a vacation. This "vacation," however, turned out to be anything but restful.

Kauai is an energy vortex, and people will tell you that strange things can happen there, especially on the night of the new moon. Although I was well aware of the fact that energy wasn't real, nor was anything that could shift and change, I still had an interest in how such things correlated to the script we appeared to act out in time and space. Indeed, my teachers had pointed out to me years ago that astrology often coincided with the script that was set up at the beginning of time. Everything in the great projection was connected, every event preordained.

On the first night on Kauai, a reader of my books who was visiting from Saudi Arabia decided to throw a party for me at a house on the North Shore. My booking agent, Jan, was in attendance along with several friends I had made the previous three years on the islands. It started to turn into a pretty rowdy affair. I remember sharing a toast with the 40 or so people who were gathered there that I'd learned from an Irish woman I knew. It went like this: "I'm not that big a drinker, one or two at most. Three, I'm under the table; and four, I'm under the host." Although it got a laugh, I'm sure a few of the attendees were surprised by the down-to-earth nature of it. Many spiritual students don't equate spirituality with having a good time.

As the night went on, my host introduced a couple of excellent belly dancers to perform. Apparently he had read about certain preferences I have, and of course I considered it to be my cultural duty to observe these dancers closely. At one point a spiritual student who was not yet familiar with *A Course in Miracles* came up to me and asked, "Are all *Course* parties this wild?" I said almost never, but I wasn't complaining.

The way the party was going didn't sit well with Karen. She said that I was staring at the dancers, and even dancing with them closely, and she was probably right. At the end of the night, we got into an argument and she left without me. I ended up spending the night at the house where the party was. I later found out that my host and the woman he lived with also had an argument that night and split up. I'm not blaming anything for this other than the fact that things happen when they're supposed to. Still, the synchronicity of it was amazing.

Karen and I got together again the next day and decided to continue the vacation. We were so used to being with each other it was hard to let go. This was painful, because the rest of the trip was a disaster. It was like torture, but without the fun.

I never let what was going on in my personal life have an effect on my public teaching. My workshop on Kauai two days later went very well, and I even made three new friends who had come to Hawaii from California. They would play into my life more and more as the months went on.

The rest of the week we spent on Kauai was a marvel of duality: so much beauty and peace, yet so much misery at the same time. Karen and I just couldn't get along. It was hard for me to remember the real purpose for this, but I tried. I remember reading a passage from the *Course* several times and giving the situation up to God:

> Bringing the ego to God is but to bring error to truth, where it stands corrected because it is the opposite of what it meets. It is undone because the contradiction can no longer stand. How long can contradiction stand when its impossible nature is clearly revealed? What disappears in light is not attacked. It merely vanishes because it is not true. Different realities are meaningless, for reality must be one. It cannot change with time or mood or chance. Its changelessness is what makes it real. This cannot be undone. Undoing is for unreality. And this reality will do for you.[15]

On Oahu, we circled the island and took in its beauty. We stayed right on the beach in the beautiful town of Kailua. We swam with dolphins, but even that didn't seem to help our situation. One night I was working on my computer, writing what would eventually become this book, and all of a sudden Karen complained from the bed that I was typing too loud. I couldn't believe it. I thought, *What's paying for us being here?* It broke my train of thought and contributed to the overall dismal picture. I also thought, *I can take responsibility for all of this, but it's still hard to understand.* Then maybe that's because the world of the ego is not always understandable. For every good there's a bad, and the only way I can understand it is to realize neither one is true. There's a true happiness beyond both the good and the bad. But that happiness isn't dependent upon what appears to be happening in the universe of time and space.

In the midst of all the strangeness, I took comfort in the support I was receiving, not just in America, but now from around the world. As my first book spread to 18 languages, I received encouragement from a wide variety of sources. In the U.S., I got to meet spiritual students every week, and this had turned out to be one of the happiest experiences of my life. I could see in their faces the difference my books and speaking were making. *Disappearance* was also receiving many accolades in print form. The positive nature of many of the comments on the Internet were especially welcome, because when the book first came out it was virtually ripped apart by so-called *Course* students whose main complaint about it seemed to be that for the most part it agreed with the teachings of Ken Wapnick, whom Arten and Pursah had described as "the *Course*'s greatest teacher." The book also made many of its own contributions, which were virtually ignored by these critics. But the supporters of the book seemed to have one reason in common for their excitement. I thought this particular reason was especially well articulated by a *Course* student and teacher named Rachel Azorre:

> As a longtime spiritual seeker as well as an experienced student and teacher of *A Course in Miracles,* I must say that this is easily the best book ever written about the *Course.* There's one test that says it all. People have been reading other books about the *Course* for 30 years. Then they go back to reading and studying the *Course* themselves or at their study groups, and they still don't understand it. I know. I've seen them and been one of them. But then this book comes along, and people are excited and reinvigorated about the *Course,* because after reading it they go back and read the *Course* or go to their study groups, and they really understand it! That's *never* happened before. Plus, new students

are coming to the *Course* with excitement and understanding. Thanks, Gary Renard, whoever you are, and your Teachers. With *The Disappearance of the Universe,* ACIM is a whole new ball game. And a lot more fun!

My workshop on Oahu, at the Diamond Head Unity Church, was especially gratifying not just because of the wonderful people but the exquisite location. I soaked up the atmosphere and the joining I could sense among those in attendance. Then, after our second week in Hawaii, Karen flew back to Maine, where she'd be returning to work, and I was off to my next adventure in San Francisco, where a big *A Course in Miracles* Conference was about to take place.

I had no idea what would await me later when I got back to Maine. I did know one thing. It wouldn't be real. As I flew away from Diamond Head and headed for the West Coast, I was more determined than ever to remember there's only one thing that's important, and this I vowed to be vigilant for. As J puts it in his unrelenting *Course:*

> His Kingdom has no limits and no end, and there is nothing in Him that is not perfect and eternal. All this is *you,* and nothing outside of this *is* you.[16]

3

THE SCRIPT IS WRITTEN, BUT NOT ETCHED IN STONE: THE NATURE OF DIMENSIONS

This is a course in how to know yourself. You have taught what you are, but have not let what you are teach you.[1]

After a few years of traveling to the major cities of North America, I'd come to the conclusion that two of them were the most beautiful. Of course, that's a personal opinion and someone else could think differently. I'd been to San Francisco twice before: once to lead a workshop in the Muir Woods for my hosts, the Community Miracles Center; and again to give a talk with my first publisher, D. Patrick Miller, whose imprint, Fearless Books, had enabled *Disappearance* to get on the map. Indeed, Patrick and I had collaborated on getting so much free publicity on the Internet and leapfrogging among spiritual websites that by the time a bigger publisher, Hay House, took over, the book was already in every Barnes & Noble in America.

On my second visit to the area, Patrick was kind enough to show me around San Francisco and also take me up to the Berkeley Hills, which offered astounding panoramic views. My new friend at the time, Gene Bogart—who had worked with Patrick by skillfully reciting one of his books as an audio CD—as well as his wife, Helen, were also with us. As we explored the area, both by land and sea, I started to appreciate some of the reasons why people love the City by the Bay.

The other city in North America I consider to be the most beautiful is Vancouver, in British Columbia. Although I certainly haven't been everywhere, Vancouver's beauty is off the charts. I remember doing my first workshop there in 2004. Intoxicated by the awesome sights, I walked with a new friend to lunch. Afterward, as we were about to leave the restaurant and go back to the workshop, my friend said, "Hey, Eckhart Tolle is in the back. Do you want to meet him?" I said, "Sure, why not?" It was a simple meeting in which my new friend introduced me to Eckhart (it turned out the two knew each other). We talked briefly about our books, and I noticed he was quite humble and unassuming. I saw nothing that would make me think he wasn't completely authentic.

What I'd later find remarkable was the way it happened. What would be the odds of going out for lunch in a city of millions of people and "accidentally" meeting Eckhart Tolle? It clearly reminded me that there's no such thing as an accident. Within a year we had both been filmed to appear in a movie called *Living Luminaries*. It wasn't a blockbuster, but it was seen by hundreds of thousands of people and helped make my work even more well known. I was then interviewed for more movies, which would be coming out in the next couple of years. One thing leads to another. And I'd go back to Vancouver just to see the city again, whether I was speaking or not.

In San Francisco I was treated like a rock star. I was wondering if the negative articles that had been written about me by three other *Course* authors would have an effect on the way people thought about me. It wasn't long before I found out. There were only three *Course* authors who would get to speak to the entire conference. I was one of them, and the other two were two of the three authors who had written the negative articles about me! They never mentioned the articles and neither did I. Of the three of us, the first speaker practically put the audience to sleep. It was then my turn. The raucous standing ovation I received before I even began to talk told me that people were basing their experience of me on their experience of my books. Indeed, although half of them knew me from my travels around the country the previous few years, the other half only knew me through my writing.

I sometimes take a show of hands to see how many people in the audience have read *Disappearance,* because it helps me know whom I'm speaking to. On this day, a good 90 percent of the people raised their hands to say they had read my first book. I gave a talk for an hour and 15 minutes, which was all I was allowed. I would have gladly spoken for five hours. I injected my smart-ass humor, which I always enjoy, into my teachings about the *Course.* The reaction I received from this crowd, both at the end of my talk and the way people would greet me in the hallways, at meals, and at my book signing, confirmed what I suspected. What was happening between most of the students of the *Course* and me was an experience of love that couldn't be affected by the opinions of others. And as the weekend went on, the conference turned into a lovefest. *Course* students who had been at odds with each other for years because of legal issues or disagreements over what the work meant were now hugging each other.

Then it struck me. What you had here was a large group of ACIM students who didn't always necessarily agree with each other about what the *Course* means, but that didn't matter! If you're a student of the *Course* and you stick with it long enough, then eventually you're bound to catch on to the fact that it's all about forgiveness. And forgiveness is all it

> **Love follows naturally from forgiveness.**

takes to lead to a lovefest. Love follows as naturally from forgiveness as, to paraphrase our friend Shakespeare, does the night from the day.

I was heartened by what I saw as a triumph of experience over theology. As the *Course* itself taught all of us at the conference: "A universal theology is impossible, but a universal experience is not only possible but necessary. It is this experience toward which the Course is directed."[2] And I could see this happening right before my eyes.

I was not only enthralled by the experience of love I felt in San Francisco (I had missed the Summer of Love in 1967), but I also realized that the wisdom contained in *A Course in Miracles* was just that—wisdom. It worked as long as people eventually remembered that it was all about forgiveness. And that was the *only* way it could really work.

I was going to make a stop in Portland, Oregon, the following weekend, and then it would be home to Maine for my birthday and a couple of days off before moving on to The Crossings in Austin, Texas. But just before I left San Francisco for Portland, I was visited once again by my favorite teachers, who seemed to enjoy using bodies to teach me not that their bodies are real, but that *no* bodies are real. It was the beginning of March, 2007, and my beautiful Pursah spoke first.

PURSAH: Hey, hotshot. Congratulations! You've been knockin' 'em alive.

ARTEN: Yes, as much as I hate to admit it, you've been decent.

GARY: Now Arten, don't get all sentimental on me.

ARTEN: Okay, then—let's talk about your marriage. What's up with *that?*

GARY: I knew you were cruel, in your own charming way.

ARTEN: Just getting to the obvious, dear brother.

GARY: All right. I already told you; I don't know what to do. I keep hanging on and so does Karen. But it's not working. So do *you* have anything to say that will help me?

ARTEN: Yes. Go home when you're supposed to, and take it from there.

GARY: I hate you. Why don't you take a hike and let me come on to Pursah?

ARTEN: I know you don't hate me, but you wouldn't mind hitting on Pursah, would you?

PURSAH: Gary, you know that as an ascended master, I'm really not interested in that sort of physical intimacy. Not that there's anything wrong with it. But my lover is God.

GARY: Come on, Pursah. It will be over in a minute, and you won't feel a thing.

PURSAH: Somehow I doubt that. But for the sake of argument, which I don't advocate, what would you say if you were *really* trying to romance me?

GARY: I'd say that if you were me and I were you, I'd love you more than I love myself. But if I were the universe and you were a galaxy, I'd consume you and then digest your essence throughout the intestines of my being.

PURSAH: I'll bet you say that to all the girls.

ARTEN: So, despite your resistance, we're going to let you go home to Karen and take it from there. And Pursah was right. Your work is going fine. We have a subject we'd like to discuss with you today, if you're up for it.

GARY: You guys usually seem to have something interesting to say. What's up? And that doesn't mean I've given up on you, Pursah.

ARTEN: Remember the time we told you that you had been practicing forgiveness enough that you avoided being in a car accident?

GARY: Yeah! I was at the movies, and I chose this sucky film and thought I made a bad decision. But later you said it got out at a different time than the one I would have chosen if I wasn't practicing forgiveness. So what happened was that because of forgiveness, there was a lesson I no longer had to learn. My learning had rendered the painful lesson unnecessary, and I switched to a different scenario. It was kind of like what the *Course* talks about early on. It mentions dimensions of time and says that the miracle, which is obviously the kind of forgiveness that comes from a place of cause and not effect, works in all the dimensions of time.[3]

ARTEN: Well, what if I told you it's not only possible for people to do that as individuals, but that it's also possible for the human race to do that as a whole?

GARY: Jesus Christ. I never thought of that. You're saying that *everything* could be altered according to what the human race thinks collectively? And when I say *altered*, I'm not saying the script can be changed, because it can't. There's something else going on when we talk about changing dimensions of time.

ARTEN: Exactly, Gary. For example, all the predictions we made about the future in our first two series of visits, plus everything we say here, could possibly become null and void if the human race were to switch to another dimension of time. If enough people practiced forgiveness, you could switch to a different scenario. And it would also be possible for the Holy Spirit to erase the old tape. Just as the Holy Spirit collapses time for an individual and renders that person further along in the overall scheme of things, the same thing can be done for the world as a whole.

PURSAH: You know how sometimes when you rent a DVD, it will contain an alternate ending? You can actually watch a different outcome to this movie you're watching, too.

GARY: Yeah! I don't really like alternate endings to movies because I like films to be works of art that are a finished product. But I wouldn't mind the human race watching something better.

PURSAH: Well, remember something: Even if you choose to watch that alternate ending, it's already been filmed! So you're *not* really changing the script; you're just watching a different part of it, and the old part is being erased. It's not that you're making the new part up as you go along—it's already there.

GARY: I see what you're saying. Like the *Course* says, you're still just reviewing something mentally that's already happened. That aspect of it never changes.

PURSAH: Yes.

GARY: So in the scenario you gave me before, it's possible that a nuclear device—and you didn't say what kind of a nuclear device, and for all I know, it could just be a dirty bomb or something—could go off in a major city. You said that four cities are the most at risk of some kind of attack: New York, Los Angeles, London, and

Tel Aviv. But now you're saying it would be possible to avoid such an attack?

PURSAH: That's correct, but notice we didn't say that you *will* avoid it. We said it's *possible* to avoid it by switching to a different scenario. Individuals as well as the human race are always determining what kind of an experience they're going to have with their own choices.

ARTEN: Now we want to caution you. Just because you practice forgiveness, it doesn't mean you'll always switch to a pleasant outcome. And *you* don't determine whether you switch dimensions of time. Only the Holy Spirit can do that, because the Holy Spirit can see the big picture and you can't. Obviously, Jesus was not given pleasant things to experience at the end of his earthly adventures, but the Holy Spirit knew he could handle it. His forgiveness was so advanced that he was healed of all guilt and thus couldn't feel any pain.

So don't always expect good things to happen. Your job is to forgive no matter what happens, and you have to learn to trust the Holy Spirit more and more as you go along. You're doing that, and you should continue. The human race as a whole must do the same. There are some major problems to be dealt with on the level of form. They're not real, and we're not here to make them real, but we can give you some advice about how to forgive these things.

GARY: When you say "these things," there's a lot that appears to be going on. You've got climate change, terrorism, and many people thinking that December 21, 2012, will be the end of the world. So I'll ask the obvious question. What's up with the 2012 thing?

ARTEN: The world isn't going to end in 2012. That would be too simple for the ego. The ego wants to keep the game going. There

Cycles repeat in different forms.

have been several times every century since the Book of Revelation when groups of people, sometimes large groups of people, have thought the world was going to end. It never does. As we've indicated to you before, 2012 is the beginning of a new cycle.

Cycles repeat in different forms. Because things have gotten bigger and faster, it will look different, but it's not *really* different. It's different in form but not content.

As for form, it will appear that America will start to better cooperate with the world in solving global problems, such as climate change. It will be difficult though, because so much time has been wasted, and the most powerful country in the world has been part of the problem instead of part of the solution. Obviously, China and India are major parts of the problem, too. And it's clear that the world's weather is becoming more and more bizarre.

GARY: You ain't kidding!

ARTEN: But before we go much further, tell us a joke. This is a heavy subject coming up, and some levity would be appropriate.

GARY: Okay. This guy sees an ad in the paper that says, "Talking dog for sale: $100." The guy's curiosity is aroused, so he calls the number and gets directions to the house where the dog is. When he shows up, the man selling the dog says, "The dog's in the other room. You can go in and talk to him if you want." So the guy goes in the room and sure enough, the dog can talk! The dog tells the man how he used to be in the CIA, and they'd send him to spy on people because no one would suspect a dog of being a spy. He was in the Kremlin spying on the Russians and fed top-secret information to the CIA, and he did all kinds of special assignments. He was considered a hero by the agency and got to retire at the same age in dog years that a person would get to retire. The agency gave him a pension, and now he's thinking about writing his memoirs.

The guy was amazed. He went out to the owner and said, "That dog can really talk! Don't you know what you've got here? You could get a million dollars. Why on earth are you selling that dog for just a hundred bucks?" And the owner says, "Ah, that dog's a liar. He never did any of those things."

PURSAH: All right, that's a cute one.

GARY: It's a true story.

ARTEN: You were starting to talk about the weather.

GARY: Oh, yeah. I first noticed it with the ice storm here nine years ago. I mean, the temperature stayed at exactly 32 degrees for days! How screwed up is that? Every telephone pole in the state had to be replaced. Literally; they all snapped. That was January of '98. Workers had to come in from all over the country to replace every pole. They did the job in a month, and they were treated like heroes. That's when I first noticed how weird the weather was getting. We lost power in the middle of the winter for 23 days. Thank God Karen's parents had a woodstove, but we were taking our lives in our hands going there. And since then we've had years where we've had record snowfalls, but last year, the winter of 2006–2007, it didn't snow at all! The ski-resort people freaked out. At the same time, New York City had its biggest one-day snowfall in history. And on Oahu, it rained for 44 days in a row! That's never happened before. It's getting biblical out there, man.

PURSAH: Speaking of weird weather, later this year it will snow in Baghdad for the first time in history. London will have its first tornado. California will get just two inches of rain. There will be a drought in both the Southeast and the Southwest, but next year there will be terrible floods in the Midwest. It's getting like it's always the same. There's either too much rain or no rain. There's either too much snow or no snow. It's either too hot or too cold. It's all extremes. "Normal" weather is disappearing. Storms will get bigger and be more damaging.

GARY: And you seem to be saying a real effort will be made by the world, with the cooperation of America, to fix the problem?

PURSAH: That's right, but it's going to be close as to whether catastrophe can be averted. You're not going to get China to cooperate. Oh, by the way, *Disappearance* will do well on the mainland of China.

GARY: Are you kidding? They won't even let it *on* the mainland. They don't like books that mention God a lot.

PURSAH: That's true, but what the Chinese Communist government really fears is any challenge to the Communist Party, and you don't do that. So eventually, they'll let your book in.

GARY: Awesome! Maybe I can go there sometime.

PURSAH: Maybe, but don't forget to consult with us and the Holy Spirit, which are the same thing, before you decide to go somewhere. You never know when it's the right time, or the safe time, to visit a country unless you ask. Are you planning on speaking in all 50 states?

GARY: Yup, I'll be up to 40 after this year.

PURSAH: Very good, but don't forget to take breaks and be good to yourself. Also, even though we've counseled you to answer questions from your critics in the past, that doesn't mean you always have to do so in the future.

NOTE: In regard to the attack articles that had been written, I wrote a response article and answered the questions that were raised. After that, Michael Mirdad, a well-known author (as well as a respected *Course* teacher) wrote an independent response to all of the articles. It was titled "A Course in Megafools" and included the following:

> For the most part, Gary recently offered his detractors, and all interested parties, a brilliant blow-by-blow defense that exposes many inconsistencies and un-truths. This defense has now been printed in *Miracles* magazine. In a human court of law, Renard would win, hands down. But it's worth mentioning here that he might have taken the high road (as did Ken Wapnick) and ignored those who would attack him. Nevertheless, his choice to respond may also bring a greater good by exposing the hypocrisies that have infiltrated the *Course in Miracles* community (mainly some of its facilitators) and thereby turned away many from studying the *Course*.

I realized that Michael was right when he said I *could* have taken the high road and ignored the people who lived in glass houses yet chose to throw stones. Not responding to my critics and not answering their questions had *not* been my guidance from Arten and Pursah; and in the past, their guidance, in general, has served me very well. However, I figured the option to overlook those who would attack me could very well be my guidance in the *future*. After all, I'd already answered all of the questions in public, and more than once. Maybe it was time for me to just relax. I found that idea very peaceful, and what Pursah had just said confirmed it for me.

GARY: Good. I've been thinking along those lines myself, but thanks for saying it. By the way, I was thinking about one of the predictions you made in *Disappearance.* You were talking to me back in the '90s. Most people don't realize it took nine years to do that book because there were so many visits and they were often far apart, especially toward the end. But you made an amazing prediction for that time because the United States was in good shape fiscally under President Clinton, and we were doing really well. But you said that America would go on the decline, and Europe would gain economic and political power. I can't believe how much the U.S. dollar has gone down the tubes since that first book came out! Some people didn't like what you said, but you were right. Maybe it's time for us to rethink some of our policies.

PURSAH: Europe is going to have its problems, too, but will eventually gain strength again. That's because America's policies aren't policies—they're calculations. They're designed to make a lot of money for the few, and the hell with everyone else. And then you can't understand why things don't work. In the case of America, it's not a question of rethinking. It's a question of thinking at all. There hasn't been any thinking for the greater good . . . but enough about politics. You have a couple of historic elections coming up, and we don't want the book to come out until after they're over.

GARY: Why's that? Are you gonna make a prediction? And doesn't that contradict what you said about more books?

PURSAH: No. There will be more books after that. But we're going to keep our other reasons to ourselves for now. In the meantime, always remember that your job is forgiveness of your world, with the help of the Holy Spirit. As far as this world is concerned, God didn't bring you to it, but the Holy Spirit will see you through it.

The Holy Spirit will see you through it.

GARY: All right, let's say the human race continues the way it is, without practicing a lot more forgiveness. What's going to happen in the dream? I mean, I know it's all for forgiveness, and these are the lessons the Holy Spirit would have me learn, but it's still interesting to get a glimpse of what's coming up.

ARTEN: If more people do *not* practice forgiveness, then these are some of the things that will happen. There will be good and bad events and developments, as always. The main difference would be that if more people *did* practice forgiveness then some of the more terrible things would *not* happen. Many dimensions of time are very similar. The differences can be few, yet major when it comes to just those few things.

GARY: Like me not getting in that car accident, except here you're talking on a bigger scale.

ARTEN: Precisely. And you're in all of these dimensions of time right now. You're living simultaneous lifetimes. You can't see it because it's walled off in the mind by the idea of separation. As we've said, you're nonspatial and nonlinear. You're everywhere, even in the illusion. But in the linear and spatial framework, you only experience a little at a time.

GARY: I'm experiencing more than I can handle already.

ARTEN: Hey, you've got it pretty good. You get to see all these places, stay in nice hotels, eat in classy restaurants. You get a lot of attention from women. By the way, how do you explain that?

GARY: It's easy. They think I'm gay.

ARTEN: Yes, that never hurts. And now that you're traveling around the world, where would you say you would find the most beautiful women?

GARY: That's easy, too. Airports.

ARTEN: Very observant.

PURSAH: Men. Could you act like grown-ups for a few minutes?

GARY: Okay, but since we're on the subject, I'm going to tell you how men think.

PURSAH: This should be good. How do men think, Gary?

GARY: It's simple. If you can't screw it, blow it up.

PURSAH: That explains a lot. Now, how about those predictions, Arten?

ARTEN: Yes, keeping in mind everything we've said, in this century you'll have many different forms of new power. In some cases these forms of power are already in limited use and will be developed further. Wind is a good example. That will become more prevalent. Also, a technology will be developed so that the process of turning coal into inexpensive gasoline, which already exists, can be done without adding even more pollution to the atmosphere. Coal is the biggest cause of problems with the climate, not cars. But when a way is found to burn coal without polluting the atmosphere, America, which has enough coal to last the next 250 years, suddenly will become the Saudi Arabia of the world. Of course you'd actually have to have an energy policy, other than making a few selected people wealthy. You'd have to develop smart ways of making power, instead of wasting your time building more nuclear power plants, as some people are advocating.

In this century, people will develop underwater energy turbines to produce unlimited clean power, and these will be driven by the Gulf Stream and other currents.

GARY: Wow. Wouldn't it be funny if someone developed that, and then the Gulf Stream stopped working because of global warming?

ARTEN: Later this century you'll have high-speed tube travel, which will revolutionize transportation.

GARY: What the hell's that?

ARTEN: We'll let you look into it. But for someone like you who travels so much, you'll wish you had it now.

PURSAH: In America, where the automobile industry has fallen into deep decline, hybrids will be the big thing. The electric car, which will be improved upon, will become popular, especially in western parts of the country. You'll even have cars that will run on compressed air.

GARY: Let's hope we don't run out of air. What about ethanol?

ARTEN: Oh yes. Only in a world where millions of people are starving to death would you take corn and turn it into fuel! It's not necessary, but just stupid enough to come into favor with your government. In the meantime, there is a way of producing unlimited energy for free, but this has been suppressed for the last century. In one dimension of time it is revealed, in another it isn't. The way people use their minds will determine what you experience.

GARY: Free energy? Holy crap! By the way, you once said that hydrogen-powered cars would catch on.

ARTEN: Yes, but we said first in Europe. America is a long way from that, and that brings up one of the scenarios. If enough people were to advance spiritually, then the forms of energy we've already mentioned would be enough to get the country into very good shape. It's up to you. If you decided to make these things work, you wouldn't *need* any other form of energy.

In the meantime, you'll have a trend toward diversification. You'll see many different kinds of cars. It's like your communications industry today. You'll see people switching from network television to the Internet and other forms of entertainment, such as the various electronic devices that are springing up. Things will never be as simple as they used to be.

GARY: Are you sure you can't tell me for certain about nuclear terrorism?

PURSAH: That wouldn't be right. Plus, don't forget that it's not *just* nuclear terrorism that's on the radar. The global nuclear threat isn't over, including with Russia and her neighbors, or even Russia and America. Then you've got North Korea and its potential targeting of South Korea and Japan, not to mention eventually Hawaii and the western United States. Then there's China. And on top of that, you've got a nuclear arms race between India and Pakistan, with China in the mix, plus Israel and Iran. It's a wild projection, dear brother.

ARTEN: Less than a year from now, a new cycle of sunspot activity will begin. This will last for five years and reach its peak in 2013. It will have an effect on everything, from the weather to human events. It's not just your atmosphere that has an influence. There are many things you can't see that help run the show, and of course it's all symbolic of something deeper: an unconscious guilt that exists at the level of the mind that can be traced all the way back to the original separation from God and the massive guilt and fear that it generated.

PURSAH: They'll find that traces of water exist on the moon, as well as ice on Mars, which means water, but much more of it. Eventually, as we've said in the past, solid evidence will be found that there was once an intelligent civilization on Mars, but it will not be known at first that they were actually your ancestors. You'll begin to colonize Mars. Scientists will eventually figure out that your DNA couldn't possibly have originated only on your planet. Wars will be fought more and more with drones in the sky and robots on the ground against people, giving the most technologically advanced side a big advantage. Members of the military will be trained in virtual boot camps.

Today, you're worried about oil. If you want to worry, what you should be concerned about is water. A shortage of fresh drinking water, as well as water to grow your crops, will become a severe problem in the future, and one you should be planning to deal with now.

ARTEN: The idea of parallel universes and multiple dimensions of time exist in several scientific theories. It's not just the metaphysicians and those into spirituality who think they exist, and they do exist within the illusion. But the nature of dimensions is not known by scientists, for when lessons are learned and these dimensions become unnecessary, they are erased by the Holy Spirit, never to be seen again. Many believe that your universe is infinite, but it's not infinite. As the *Course* teaches, through the Holy Spirit, there were limits put on your ability to miscreate.[4] And all will eventually accept the truth. As J also teaches, "The acceptance of the Atonement by everyone is only a matter of time. This may appear to contradict free will because of the inevitability of the final decision, but this is not so."[5]

> **If we choose to stay here, the outcome is always eventually death.**

GARY: So the only free will we *really* have as prisoners in the illusion is the ability to choose the Holy Spirit, which frees us, instead of the ego, which imprisons us. If we choose to stay here, the outcome is always eventually death. But if we choose to go home, the outcome is eternal life.

PURSAH: Excellent. Also, in the future scientists will be able to generate organs that will match your body and be immune to rejection, and make a heart beat again that was thought to be dead for too long. And scientists, as well as others, will begin to think more and more of not only the Earth, but also the entire universe, as a living organism. They'll see that stellar embryos give birth to stars, and that even though various entities do not always breathe oxygen like humans, that certainly doesn't mean they're not just as "alive" as humans.

And if that's not enough, this is the century when confirmed contact will be made with extraterrestrials. That's already happened, but it hasn't been publicly confirmed by your scientists.

ARTEN: By the way, you made a mistake in the last book. Remember when we showed you your thousands of different bodies, and then at the end you were hoping to see what Arten looked like in this lifetime?

PURSAH: Well, we didn't let you see that person. Then you wanted to go back and see what Thomas and Thaddaeus looked like. In the book, you have yourself saying, "Can you go back one more?" in order to accomplish this. Of course we knew what you really wanted because we can read your mind, and we showed you Thomas and Thaddaeus. But if we had just gone back one more you wouldn't have seen them. You had about 20 other lifetimes between them, including the American Indian one with the Great Sun, the one as Roger Sherman, and the one where you died at the Alamo.

NOTE: I've learned from visions, memories, dreams, and also from renowned psychics that in previous lifetimes, I was a man named William Harrison from Ohio, who was killed at the Alamo; as well as Roger Sherman, one of the signers of the Declaration of Independence and a highly respected congressman from Connecticut who helped establish the American government. The renowned trance medium Kevin Ryerson, made famous by Shirley MacLaine in her book and movie *Out on a Limb,* confirmed through his spirit guide, the Ascended Master Ahtun Re, that I was indeed both Roger Sherman and Saint Thomas in other lifetimes.

GARY: Yes, as one of those politicians might say, I misspoke myself.

ARTEN: Now we have a tough one for you. This has been speculated about by others, so it's not an entirely new idea. But most people don't know it, and even if they've heard it, they don't know for sure if it's true, so we have to tell you the truth.

GARY: All right. You sound serious.

ARTEN: Parts of the United States government were actively involved in the attacks on the World Trade Center, the Pentagon, and the four hijacked planes that resulted in the deaths of nearly 3,000 Americans and people from other countries on September 11, 2001.

GARY: You didn't just say what I think you said.

ARTEN: Yes, I'm sorry. But it's not like there isn't plenty of evidence of it. The Twin Towers didn't collapse because of the planes striking them and the fire. No skyscraper has ever collapsed that way because of fire. The buildings were imploded, like when they bring down an old hotel in Las Vegas. The hijackers were duped by the CIA into thinking they were acting under the orders of their terrorist organization, when they were really being used by the CIA. They did exactly what the CIA wanted them to do, and they ended up playing their part, *thinking* they were being directed by their own leaders. With communications risky, it wasn't that hard for them to be used in this manner. Plus, the hijackers weren't the same people your government said they were. And the planes that went into the World Trade Center were not the hijacked planes. They were empty planes that were guided by remote control.

Al-Qaeda did not organize the attacks and neither did Osama bin Laden, although he was happy to eventually take the credit for it. He was the perfect murderer for the government to have as the fall guy.

Do some research. Listen to what thousands of individual physicists and engineers say about what happened at the World Trade Center, the 7 World Trade Center building, and the Pentagon. Don't listen to organizations. The truth is that members of your own government, particularly the Vice President—who just happened to be in charge of air defense around Washington,

D.C., that morning—wanted a "Pearl Harbor" to occur in order to allow the government to gain power over its own people and do whatever it pleased throughout the world. You've seen some of the results, including using the aftermath as an excuse for even more surveillance of American citizens and a big step toward fascism.

President Bush wasn't told about it, as the perpetrators had a role for him to play also. The people who committed these major crimes against humanity, who believe they're intelligent, thought that Iraq would be an easy victory. They were wrong. And they're also wrong to think the evidence won't eventually convince people of the truth. That, however, is a long way off.

Yes, there are people who already know the truth, but most of the American public are sheep who believe whatever they hear on the corporate-owned news. The corporations and national governments are in turn controlled by banking powers such as the Federal Reserve Board and Central Banks that are owned by the most powerful families on Earth. These are the individuals who want global domination.

The real Achilles' heel in the 9/11 illusion is building 7. It was imploded later in the day. The building was struck by no planes, was a football field away from the World Trade Center, and just happened to house the headquarters of the CIA in New York City. The evidence of the CIA's involvement had to be destroyed; however, the super thermites used to implode the buildings were *not* completely annihilated. Traces were found at the scene. And the heat and energy created by these super thermites was measured after the crime. There was far more energy present at the scene than could have been generated by the scenario presented by the government and rubber-stamped by the congressional investigation.

GARY: Why didn't you tell me this before?

ARTEN: Think, Gary. You weren't ready. Our last visit to you in the first series was soon after 9/11. You had a lot to do the next year and a half just to get the first book out there. You were in shock like the rest of the country. And we wouldn't have been doing you any favors at the time by having you put out a book that accused your own government of planning and participating in 9/11. It would have brought scorn on you and completely distracted everyone from the message of the book.

GARY: How could the animals that did this pull it off without people knowing about it?

ARTEN: Four CIA agents, acting as maintenance personnel, only needed a few weeks to plant the thermites, which were detonated by radio signal. Super thermites, the kind that were used, are not overly bulky. They are smaller, more advanced, and much more powerful than other thermites.

Just sit with this, and eventually try to forgive it. It's all still the same projection it always was, Gary. Try to look through it and see the reality of spirit.

GARY: All right, but this *is* a tough one. Forget about a few years ago—I don't even know if I'm ready for it now.

PURSAH: Remember, don't make it real. Just notice it and then forgive it. It's like you're watching a virtual-reality video game, and there's no one else in the room. It's just you. There isn't really anyone else with you, except the Holy Spirit, and there's not really anyone on the screen. And what you're seeing is not true.

And with that we should temporarily disappear. We love you, Gary. Keep your chin up and keep on forgiving. You honor us. Choose the miracle of forgiveness. For as J teaches you:

> Reality belongs only to spirit, and the miracle acknowledges only truth.[6]

4

BODILY HEALING FOR
AN ENLIGHTENED MIND

*God did not make the body, because it is destructible, and
therefore not of the Kingdom. The body is the symbol of what
you think you are. It is clearly a separation device, and therefore
does not exist. The Holy Spirit, as always, takes what you have
made and translates it into a learning device. Again as always,
He reinterprets what the ego uses as an argument for separation
into a demonstration against it. If the mind can heal the
body, but the body cannot heal the mind, then the mind must
be stronger than the body. Every miracle demonstrates this.*[1]

I wanted to talk with Arten and Pursah more about the subject of
healing. My understanding was that when I practiced forgiveness, I *was* doing a healing. But I didn't know if I always needed to
have a specific intention to heal a particular problem in a person,
or whether a more general approach was better. I've had some experience in successfully healing my own back pain. It's been several years since my back had gone out, and I was hoping it never
would again. I developed a specific thought process several years
before to deal with my own back pain and even adapted it a few

months earlier to handle the problem with my right radial nerve and hand. It worked very well, and I wanted to talk to my teachers about that.

I knew there was nothing wrong with using what *A Course in Miracles* would refer to as "magic." Magic is when you try to heal an illusion by using other illusions—for example, trying to heal pain by using medicine or surgery. Those methods are often necessary for people to be healed. If they were healed spontaneously without magic, their ego may become too fearful and find an even worse way to hurt them. There's nothing wrong with throwing the ego a bone once in a while, especially if you know you're doing it. Besides, everything in the illusion is magic. Water is magic. Oxygen is magic. It doesn't mean you don't use them while you appear to be here.

When the first day of spring 2007 rolled around, I had a feeling it was about that time. Arten and Pursah had been appearing before me monthly, and I always looked forward to it. That didn't necessarily mean they'd always appear monthly in the future, but I had a feeling they were about to.

When I had returned home from the *Course* conference in San Francisco the day before my birthday, things between Karen and me went from bad to worse. It was probably the most terrible birthday of my life. Karen always cared a lot about birthdays, but it was clear she no longer cared about mine. I sensed our marriage was definitely over, yet I was so busy I didn't know when I'd have time to do anything about it. I decided that when Arten and Pursah showed up again, I wanted to talk about the body and healing, and concentrate mostly on that subject. They were happy to go along with me.

PURSAH: So you've been thinking about the thought process you developed and used with the Holy Spirit's guidance on your back, and then recently you adapted it to help your hand. Why don't you give us the back process first? Some of your readers could use it to help themselves. Then we'll get to your hand and how similar thoughts can be transferred to almost any healing challenge.

GARY: I like it when you get right to the point. This thought process is based on the *Course* as well as a couple of things you guys said in the *Disappearance* chapter called "Healing the Sick." I'm gonna talk to you as if you're the one who's in pain. That way people who read it will be able to use the process if they want to. I think this can help with any kind of chronic pain. Of course, everyone on the level of form is unique, and different right-minded ideas work best for different people.

This is meant to be done when you go to bed at night. It will put your mind into a healing mode. Then, when you sleep, your mind will work on healing the body. The Holy Spirit plays the most important role, and it would be helpful if you thought about the Holy Spirit and joined with It just before doing this process. Think of the Holy Spirit again before you nod off. Don't be heavy about it. Just invite the Holy Spirit to join with you.

First, when you lie down, think about the painful area and remind yourself that pain, as well as your body itself, is a mental process. Pain is not a physical process. You're the one who's thinking this pain in your dream. It's not real pain; it's a dream of pain, and you're the dreamer. The pain is in your mind, just like the entire dream is. And if it's in your mind, you can change your mind about it. Then, once you're very clear that it's a mental process, tell yourself the same thing the *Course* says, "The guiltless mind cannot suffer."[2] After a couple of minutes, when you're very clear about that, then tell yourself: *I'm innocent, and God loves me unconditionally. All God wants to do is take care of me forever, because God knows I'm just as innocent as God Itself.* Picture yourself joining with God and extending into infinity. You're unlimited, free of the body, and totally taken care of by God.

Now visualize the beautiful, pristine, white light of the Holy Spirit coming to you and surrounding you. In a minute or two, this healing light is not only all around you, but it's also all the way through you. The love of the Holy Spirit is absolving you of any unconscious guilt you may not be aware of, and you can have confidence you will be healed. You're not alone in this. The Holy Spirit has found you innocent. Then when you're ready, you can go to sleep in the healing love of spirit.

Do this for 30 nights, and be open to the possibility that all sickness and pain are of the mind and have nothing to do with the body.[3]

ARTEN: Very good. You simply thought of your back when you originally used that process, and it worked; and a few months ago, you thought of your hand, and more specifically, your nerves all the way from your neck and shoulder down through your arm and hand. And it worked again for you.

GARY: Yeah, pretty good, huh?

ARTEN: Not bad for one of those *Course* people. Have you tried to heal anyone else lately?

GARY: Well, there were two people, one in New York City and the other in Phoenix, who I know were healed. One openly said so, and the other wouldn't admit it. Of course it wasn't really me who healed them. It's always the mind of the patient that decides to get well, usually in the unconscious.

Then there was this young woman at one of my workshops, and she couldn't sit still. I noticed during the break she walked around really fast. In fact, she did everything fast. I think she had some type of hyperactive disorder. Anyway, I joined with her at the level of the mind and told her how innocent she was and practiced forgiveness with her.

PURSAH: Did it work?

GARY: I don't know. She was still moving pretty fast at the end there. But that doesn't mean it didn't work soon after the workshop, right?

PURSAH: That's true. And besides, after you practice healing and forgiveness, you should leave it in the Holy Spirit's hands and let it go. You should have no attachment to the outcome, just like everything else in this world.

GARY: I guess if I want to do the *Course* perfectly, all I have to do is give up the world, or at least any psychological attachment to anything here.

PURSAH: That's right. Are you ready?

GARY: I'd like to think so.

PURSAH: Don't worry about it. Just keep practicing. You're doing fine, and I think you did help that girl at your workshop.

GARY: I hope so. Hey, imagine having obsessive-compulsive behavior and attention deficit disorder at the same time? I'll bet that's a bitch.

PURSAH: We're going to suggest some things you can do to help your ego with your health.

GARY: Are you suggesting I use magic?

ARTEN: Think of these things as *preferences*. As long as you appear to be in a body, you're going to do things that bodies appear to do. Just because you're a *Course* student, it doesn't mean you don't exercise or brush your teeth. So we're going to give you a few suggestions to help your ego improve your health. As long as you're not overly driven by these things, they can be fun.

> **As long as you appear to be in a body, you're going to do things that bodies appear to do.**

PURSAH: All right. This can especially be fun for couples. Arten and I used this both for fun and for health reasons. It can be very relaxing.

GARY: This sounds good.

PURSAH: There are five areas of the body that are often neglected but that hold a *lot* of nerve endings. Stimulating these nerves promotes well-being throughout the body. These areas should be rubbed and massaged. If you don't have anyone to do it for you, then you should do it yourself.

GARY: Kinky. Where do I start? Of course, I'd rather have you do it.

PURSAH: You start with number one: **the scalp.** There are so many nerves there that, especially if someone else is massaging you and getting into it, you'll sometimes feel sensations in different parts of your body. It's very good for you. Make sure the whole scalp gets done. It's a good way to maintain physical health. The movement you do when washing your hair isn't enough— massage with your fingers and palms.

The second area to stimulate is **the ears.** This area, like the scalp, is usually ignored by healers and massage therapists, yet once again, you have clusters of nerve endings there. Plus, having your ears, especially the inner parts, massaged feels so *good.*

And then we have number three: **the heart.**

GARY: The heart. That's interesting. It's also kind of funny because I read about how a doctor will sometimes massage someone's heart *after* it stops beating. But you're saying it would be a good idea to massage it *before* it stops beating.

PURSAH: Very important. And once again, the heart is almost totally neglected. Yet massaging and stimulating it would help it to heal itself. It helps circulate the blood better and keep the arteries clearer. With heart disease being the number one cause of death on the level of form, it would make a big difference to follow our advice on this.

GARY: Makes sense to me. What's next?

PURSAH: You'll like this one. The fourth area is **the navel.** The navel is also the point of numerous nerve endings that connect throughout the middle of the body, from your chest to your private parts. And the belly button is also usually very neglected.

GARY: Tell me about it.

PURSAH: And if you enjoy any of these forms of healing at the same time that you're being healed, don't feel guilty. All of which brings us to the fifth and final but also very important part of the body to be massaged and stimulated: **the feet.**

GARY: I had reflexology once at the spa at The Crossings, and it was great! Yeah, it hurt in certain places, but a lot of it felt wonderful.

PURSAH: In all of these places, there may be certain areas that hurt a little when they're stimulated. What I've just described is basically reflexology for the entire body, not just the feet. Yes, you include the feet. And just like reflexology, if you continue with it, the pain will eventually go away. It hurts because there's something wrong in the part of the body that the nerves correspond to. But the stimulation of the nerves eventually causes that area to be healed, much like acupuncture. Then in time, upon continued stimulation, if there's no longer any pain, then it means the corresponding part of the body that had something wrong with it has now been healed. And just like it teaches in the Psychotherapy section of the *Course,* you practice forgiveness at the same time you're doing this—maybe not every second, but at least every now and then.

GARY: Very cool. And what if there isn't any pain?

PURSAH: Then enjoy. An ounce of prevention is worth a pound of cure.

GARY: Thanks! I'm gonna use this. Any other pointers?

ARTEN: Yes, don't forget the basics. You may think, *Why should it matter if I do healthy things when it's my thoughts that run everything?* The answer is simple. You're trying to educate your ego. Your ego wants you to think you're a body. You want your ego to be undone so you can go home to what you really are. In order to help the ego relax and allow itself to be undone, you do some bodily things while you appear to be here. And you know what? You'd have to do that anyway! If you just sit on a park bench and meditate for the rest of your life, you're still going to have to eat eventually. Even J ate food, had normal relationships, and communicated with people.

The bottom line is that when it comes to your seeming existence here, you should do things that make sense. And eventually you'll get to the point on your spiritual path where it doesn't make any difference because by thinking those right-minded thoughts, you'll get totally in touch with your experience of spirit all the time. But it's a process. Allow yourself that process.

GARY: So you're saying that along the way, as I'm practicing forgiveness and my ego is undone, I should take care of myself at the same time. And that will result in a healthy body?

ARTEN: Maybe.

GARY: Maybe?

ARTEN: Remember, this is to help you live a good life while you appear to be here and help you undo your ego at the same time. But you can't be attached to outcomes or else you're making the whole thing real. People want to attach a value to everything, including bodies, and they don't realize it's all subjective. If they're on a spiritual path, then they *assume* that it's more spiritual to have a healthy body than a sick body. But is it? There are athletes who have the healthiest bodies in the world, but they're not necessarily spiritually mature. On the other hand, there are very spiritual people who have sick bodies. The truth is that when you were going to get sick was already determined before you ever appeared to come here, just like everything else.

GARY: Then how can I judge what's spiritual?

ARTEN: Exactly.

PURSAH: There is a narrow door you can walk through, if you're willing to, and it is this: *A truly spiritual attitude would be that there isn't any difference between having a healthy body or a sick body.* Why? Because neither one is true.

GARY: Then why should I try to have a healthy body?

ARTEN: The answer is why not? Remember, I said this was a *preference*, not a rule. You become attached to rules and religions, but with a preference you don't have to be attached to an outcome. It's a choice that you make. But it's not something you're overzealous about. You can lighten up and enjoy life, and be prepared to forgive no matter what appears to happen.

> **A truly spiritual attitude would be that there isn't any difference between having a healthy body or a sick body.**

GARY: So people have all kinds of value judgments, such as it's better to be healthy than sick, and it's better to have a beautiful body than a body that people may consider to be not so beautiful. But who said what's beautiful? It's all made up. Like people assume a human body must be more valuable than an animal body, especially since we eat them, or at least a lot of us do; and the rest of us eat plants, which are also alive and can respond to our thoughts and words. But I've seen a lot of evidence lately, especially on video, that animals have the ability to think much more than what people previously believed. So say an animal is going through life seeing with love? I could see love, feelings, and intelligence behind the eyes of my dog. And if what J said is true in that as you see him you will see yourself . . . then wouldn't that mean my dog was making spiritual progress?

PURSAH: Yes, she was. And she'll be in Heaven with you just like everyone else, not as a body, but as what she really is: the same as you, which is spirit. And you'll sense her presence in the oneness, so you won't miss her, because you'll experience that everyone and everything is there, which would by definition include every person and every animal you ever loved.

The values people have are rooted in the world, but the true value that everyone has is not of this world. The Holy Spirit also works with animals, who have their own way of thinking from species to species. Like people, they make spiritual progress—or not—from lifetime to lifetime. And like people, they're all going to the same place with you. Christianity doesn't believe that animals have a soul, but the truth is that mind is mind, and it doesn't matter what the container appears to be.

GARY: Yeah, and I like what you said about how healthy or sick doesn't really matter because neither one is true. I take it the same thing would apply to money. I remember my parents felt very guilty because they didn't have any money. And since my books have come out, I've met a lot of people who feel very guilty because they have so much money. You can't win. People will feel guilty because they don't have any money, and they'll feel guilty because they have too much. They'll feel guilty for any reason at all! We need to give ourselves a break. We have to realize *it doesn't matter* if you're rich, and it doesn't matter if you're poor because neither one is true. And if neither one is true, then neither one can be more spiritual than the other.

PURSAH: Bravo. Today it's fashionable to think it's very spiritual to be rich. So if you get a billion dollars, you think it's because you've used your mind to attract it, when the truth is it was just your turn. It would have happened anyway because that's the way the script was written, and the way you thought and everything else that seemed to occur was part of the script. You know, a hundred years ago it was considered very spiritual to be poor. Some people would even take a vow of poverty! That's why we say it's all subjective. Fads come and go, but real spirituality remains the same. The right idea is to have a kind of spirituality where you can be happy and peaceful no matter *what* comes your way. That's freedom, and that's authentic spirituality.

ARTEN: Getting back to the task of exercising certain preferences while you appear to be here, and practicing forgiveness at the same time, I'm going to give you a simple list of things you can do to keep your ego mind occupied while you slip in your right-minded thoughts simultaneously:

#1. *Walk.* You can start with 30 minutes a day, which would be about a mile and a half. The average person walks three miles per hour. But you eventually want to work your way up to an hour, which would be three miles per day. It's okay to take two days off a week if you feel like it, but you don't have to. Still, five days a week is enough.

GARY: Yeah. I remember reading a story where John Travolta started walking every day for an hour, and after three years he had lost 39 pounds or something. And unlike with a lot of diets, if you continue walking, you'll keep the weight off instead of gaining it back.

ARTEN: That's right. You used to take your dog walking a lot, right?

GARY: I think she took me. But yeah, I've gained about 15 pounds since she made her transition.

ARTEN: It's all about habits, just like with the miracle. You get used to doing something so much that you miss it if you don't do it. Aside from walking, you should also do this:

#2. *Breathe deeply.* This is vital. Whenever you think of it, take a deep breath. And exhale deeply, too. You want to get the used air out of your diaphragm and the new air in. You'll find that when you're tired if you breathe deeply for a while, you'll feel more energetic.

#3. *Stretch.* Stretch your legs and back and arms. Stay loose.

GARY: It's better to be elastic than plastic.

ARTEN: #4. *Drink <u>a lot</u> of water.* People who drink a lot of water don't get cancer as often as people who don't. This is important for both men and women. In women, it sometimes helps prevent breast cancer. Of course, it's the mind that decides to get sick or get well, but since your body is mostly water anyway, this helps prevent it from becoming more dense. Enough water also helps prevent headaches.

#5. *Fast one day per month.* Take one day a month and don't eat. It's okay to drink juices that day, but no food, no booze, and no drugs.

GARY: No drugs? Forget it.

ARTEN: Seriously, statistics show significantly fewer heart attacks in people who fast one day a month, for whatever reason. Some Mormons do it as part of their religion, and although it's not the reason why they do it, studies have shown that it has healthy benefits.

#6. *Eat honey.* You don't have to eat it every day, but honey is one of the most overlooked wonders on the level of form. Archaeologists have discovered honey from Egyptian excavations that is thousands of years old, and it's still fresh! Honey is as close as you'll come to finding something on the level of form that is both organic and virtually indestructible. If you have trouble sleeping, instead of taking a sleeping pill, take two tablespoonfuls of honey before you go to bed, or as much as you can take up to that amount. You might be surprised. You've read about people who have died by combining prescription medications because they were desperate for sleep. If they knew about the healing properties of honey, that wouldn't happen.

If you have heartburn, take honey a half an hour before you eat dinner or before you go out to eat. Then do it again before you go to bed. Keep it up, and it has a good chance of working. But there are two things to remember: No one thing works for everyone, because the ego can be very complicated at the level of the unconscious. All of these things have a good chance of working for most people though. Also, never give honey to children under three years old. Their bodies aren't developed enough for it yet.

In addition, if you have allergies, consume honey that comes from the area that you live in.

#7. *Drink noni juice.* It doesn't taste so good, but it's not as bad if you refrigerate it, which you're supposed to do after you open it anyway. Extracted from the noni plant, mostly in Tahiti, it has many healing properties. You've had memories of being a kahuna in Hawaii, right?

GARY: Yes! Especially in my dreams. I taught and practiced the Huna religion, performed healings, and used the noni plant for many reasons—such as on wounds externally and the juice for internal problems. I had a few good lifetimes on the Hawaiian Islands. That was part of it. I'll have to get back into some of these things, even if it's just for fun.

ARTEN: #8. *Drink juices.* Whether it's orange juice, tomato juice, grape juice, grapefruit juice, carrot juice, nectars, or whatever, it's all good. If people can't afford or can't stand noni juice, they can substitute other juices. If they made it a point to have one or two glasses of fruit juice every day, it would make a difference on the level of the body. Of course, a decent diet is helpful, too. Don't avoid vegetables. It's better to eat the few vegetables you like than to not eat any at all. In a restaurant, instead of the bread, have a salad. Little habits add up.

#9. *Go out in the sun for 20 minutes a day when it's sunny, and take vitamin D_3.* Those two things combined will help prevent a lot of problems, including depression, although we know it's really thought that causes these things. But these suggestions will help you feel good, and if you feel good, you're more likely to remember to apply the right thoughts. The better you think, the better you'll feel. And the better you feel, the better you'll think, especially if you have a discipline like the *Course* to guide you.

#10. *Laugh.* Rent comedies or watch highlights of good comedy TV shows. Go to funny movies or a comedy club. Laughter is better than any other form of medicine.

#11. *If you want to stay young, look into age extension.* That's the wave of the future: finding natural products that can stimulate your body's ability to heal itself and stay young. Eventually, you'll make an age-extension product, called MaxOne, available to people. Just do that one. We don't want you selling things that aren't directly related to the *Course,* but we'll make an exception for it. It's part of the wave of the future I'm talking about, and it's very easy to use.

Vitamin supplements, especially vitamin C, have served you well. Keep it up, Gary. There are also supplements that prevent inflammation. This is very important. Most Americans have some clogged arteries from fat and sugar consumption, but it doesn't usually cause harm unless there is inflammation. This constricts the arteries, making them easier to become blocked. Since you've been researching vitamins for 30 years, we'll let you find the right supplement to prevent this on your own.

Incidentally, intravenous doses of vitamin C are being used successfully in some parts of the world to cure most kinds of cancer. It's very difficult in North America to find places that do this, because most things that work are not allowed by the medical industry. They don't make money curing people; they make money treating sick people. It's up to individuals to do their own research and take responsibility for their own health.

#12. *Oxygenate your body.* This last one is a little tricky, as it takes some discipline, so most people won't do it. You have to do it right and follow instructions. It's essential to your health to realize that the lack of oxygen is the most overlooked problem in the human body. A cancer cell cannot live in the presence of oxygen. If you could properly oxygenate all of the cells in your body, then most diseases would be prevented, or cured if you have one.

The best way to oxygenate the body is through the ingestion of 35 percent food-grade hydrogen peroxide. This is not to be confused with the 3 percent stuff that dentists and doctors use, which *cannot* be ingested without potential harm. There is a regimen that can be followed to oxygenate the body properly with the 35 percent food-grade hydrogen peroxide. The best information about it is in a little book called *The One Minute Cure,* by Madison Cavanaugh. As we said, the instructions must be followed to the letter, and most people won't do it because they don't have the discipline. But if you do, it's one of the most powerful things on the level of form that you can possibly do for your health. Don't take too much. It's taken by putting drops of it into water. Follow the instructions.

That's it, buddy. Nothing strenuous. In fact, most of these things are fun and easy, but like the *Course,* they can't work for you if you don't do them.

GARY: A lot of people have told me I should do yoga, but I was thinking it might get in the way of my beer.

PURSAH: If you like yoga and want to stick to it, that's great, but you're not usually the kind of person who's into physical discipline, so walking may be best for you. The *Course* discipline is something you do as you go along living your so-called life, which is ideal for you. So we'll leave the yoga and other decisions up to you to decide with the Holy Spirit. There's no doubt that yoga and many other approaches are very positive forces in the lives of many people, even if they do make the body real.

ARTEN: We've given you some preferences. Pursah and I did these things in our last lifetime together—the one where we achieved enlightenment. These are not the reasons *why* we became enlightened. That was accomplished by applying the discipline of the Holy Spirit's thought system. But these practices *are* fun and helpful, so enjoy!

GARY: Thanks, Arten. You know you're not that bad of a guy for a tall, dark, handsome, Greek god–looking kind of a person.

ARTEN: I knew that was why you didn't like me. I'm glad to see you're forgiving it.

GARY: Anything else?

PURSAH: In your case, there wouldn't be anything wrong with getting enough rest. You've got to remember that it's okay to say no. You've been so enthusiastic about sharing our message that you don't take enough time for yourself. Learn from Edgar Cayce. He worked himself to death! He felt a responsibility to help everyone who came to his door.

They are spirit, the same as God, and that can never change.

You need to stop and smell the flowers. If you can't say no to the requests of others, then you haven't yet overcome egocentricity. You're making it real. You're saying, "That's a real body with a real problem, and I've got to help." It totally misses the point.

They're *not* bodies, they *don't* have a real problem, and they're *not* there. They are spirit, the same as God, and that can never change. As the *Course* teaches, the body isn't even alive:

> Everything is accomplished through life, and life is of the mind and in the mind. The body neither lives nor dies, because it cannot contain you who are life.[4]

It also says:

> For it is not the body that is like the Son's Creator. And what is lifeless cannot be the Son of Life.[5]

Gary: Hey, that reminds me of the first bumper sticker I saw when I visited California. It was on a hearse. It said: I SEE DEAD PEOPLE.

ARTEN: Try to remember the uncompromising distinctions J makes in his *Course.* For as he says, "There is no life outside of Heaven. Where God created life, there life must be."[6]

We're going to leave you by reciting a quotation from the *Course* that we want you to think about for a while. You can look it up later. You'll find it easily.

GARY: Do you remember the first book? I had to find *all* the quotes from the *Course* on my own. I didn't even have a *Concordance!* Today, everybody just types in a phrase on their computer from the electronic version of the *Course,* and they can find any quote they want in an instant.

PURSAH: Your way served you well when it came to learning the *Course.* So the quote we want you to think about is as follows. When you feel down because of your personal relationship situation, think of us, and J, and forgive the world as we did.

> The ego uses the body to conspire against your mind, and because the ego realizes that its "enemy" can end them both merely by recognizing they are not part of you, they join in the attack together. This is perhaps the strangest perception of all, if you consider what it really involves. The ego, which is not real, attempts to persuade the mind, which *is* real, that the mind is the ego's learning device; and further, that the body is more real than the mind is. No one in his

right mind could possibly believe this, and no one in his right mind does believe it.

Hear, then, the one answer of the Holy Spirit to all the questions the ego raises: You are a child of God, a priceless part of His Kingdom, which He created as part of Him. Nothing else exists and only this is real. You have chosen a sleep in which you have had bad dreams, but the sleep is not real and God calls you to awake. There will be nothing left of your dream when you hear Him, because you will awaken. Your dreams contain many of the ego's symbols and they have confused you. Yet that was only because you were asleep and did not know. When you wake you will see the truth around you and in you, and you will no longer believe in dreams because they will have no reality for you. Yet the Kingdom and all that you have created there will have great reality for you, because they are beautiful and true.[7]

5

LESSONS OF THOMAS AND THADDAEUS

I have been correctly referred to as "the lamb of God who taketh away the sins of the world," but those who represent the lamb as blood-stained do not understand the meaning of the symbol. Correctly understood, it is a very simple symbol that speaks of my innocence. The lion and the lamb lying down together symbolize that strength and innocence are not in conflict, but naturally live in peace. "Blessed are the pure in heart for they shall see God" is another way of saying the same thing. A pure mind knows the truth and this is its strength. It does not confuse destruction with innocence because it associates innocence with strength, not with weakness.[1]

Ever since Arten and Pursah completed their first series of visits at the end of 2001, I've had more and more memories of previous lifetimes, as well as a few glimpses of my future, final lifetime. These memories come in different forms. Most of my mystical experiences have been very visual and could happen at any time during the day. I could be meditating and see images or visions. But the most common time for me to see images with messages is when I'm in what I would call the "in-between zone," that point where I'm still awake in bed at night but just about to doze off to sleep.

Not really asleep and not really awake, I'd often see images in those few moments. These images could take many different forms, but sometimes they'd be more than just still pictures. They'd occasionally develop into complete scenes of other places and times, often with sound. It was very much like watching a movie. As the years went on, the images became stronger and clearer. My feeling was that even though I could also have such experiences in my deep-dreaming phase of sleep, the most accurate visions as well as the easiest ones to remember occurred at that point where the unconscious mind was rising to the surface and met a relaxed conscious mind. It's the information from the unconscious mind that's the most reliable, and as it rises to the surface, those who can view it the most accurately have already learned how to get their conscious mind out of the way.

In my case this was accomplished by being half asleep. In the case of Edgar Cayce, he simply went completely to sleep, and his unconscious mind spoke through him—thus, he was called the "Sleeping Prophet." The best channelers, psychics, and mediums in history have been the ones who found a way to limit the conscious mind's ability to interfere with the unconscious. The conscious mind acts as a filter that inflicts the person's ego on the interpretation of the information. The less conscious mind you have filtering the information, the better the quality of the message.

One example of this would be Jane Roberts, who channeled Seth. She'd let go of her conscious mind altogether and let another being come completely through her. The best medium I ever saw is George Anderson, and he keeps his conscious mind occupied by doodling in a sketchbook. The accuracy of the information that comes out of his unconscious mind is amazing. He doesn't have to ask people questions the way most psychics and mediums do. He simply gives his clients a steady stream of information that astounds them.

I usually get my conscious mind out of the way by meditating or almost sleeping. Yes, I would sometimes see visions when I appeared to be wide-awake, and I was always awake when I saw Arten and Pursah. But the information that came from them wasn't just from my unconscious mind—it was also coming from manifesta-tions of the Holy Spirit, just as the Voice of the *Course* was a mani-festation of the Holy Spirit.

As for my past-life recall, I re-alized that these lifetimes were se-rial dreams, and that the only real value they had was to learn how to use them for forgiveness, especial-ly since those same forgiveness les-

I realized that these lifetimes were serial dreams.

sons were being presented to me again in this lifetime. The form may be different, but the lesson and the meaning are the same.

As we are learning these lessons, it's wise to remember that even reincarnation is an illusion, because we never actually incar-nate into a body. Our experience is what Einstein called an "opti-cal delusion of consciousness." Yes, it looks and feels like we're in a body, but this is a trick of the ego, a false experience. The body is not real; it's just a part of the same projection as the rest of the universe.

As to how I recalled these dream lifetimes, *most* of these mem-ories came when I was in bed. That is, until the fifth visit of this series by my teachers.

NOTE: For those who aren't familiar with the differences, a *psychic* generally deals with minds that appear to be incarnate, although not always, while a *medium* deals exclusively with minds that have made their transition to the "other side." Channelers have other beings speak through them. Helen Schucman was prob-ably the greatest channeler who ever lived because of the quality of information she delivered, and she was very unique in the sense that she didn't have to alter her consciousness in order for Jesus to clearly communicate through her. But her conscious mind was distracted by "seeing" the words Jesus spoke to her, and by her writing them down in her own particular brand of shorthand. However, because she became known as simply "hearing" Jesus's voice, she set off a wave of copycat channelers who claimed they were channeling Jesus without ever understanding the amount of filtering they were doing.

This is why the quality and consistency of Helen's information from Jesus was so much better than others. Although other channelers often think they are saying "the same thing" as *A Course in Miracles*, they seldom understand all of the distinctions nor can they see where they've gone off message by including information they personally believe. Many of them made up their own versions of the *Course,* thinking they were an improvement or a continuation of the *Course,* when the truth is that they would have been better off learning the original rather than making up another one. The information they were channeling was being filtered by their own egos. Why not stick with the real thing?

To review, in the previous years I'd had vivid memories of a lifetime as a member of the Pharaoh's family in ancient Egypt, as well as Judas Didymus Thomas, now called Saint Thomas. And as previously stated, I also experienced lifetimes as a Native American from Cahokia who knew the extraordinary teacher "The Great Sun"; a signer of the Declaration of Independence named Roger Sherman; a man from Ohio who was killed at the Alamo named William Harrison; and my future lifetime as one of my own teachers. But I had also experienced numerous memories in the form of visions from other lifetimes where I could not yet identify the names of the people I had been at that time, or the people I knew then, although sometimes I could.

It was early on a Tuesday afternoon when I saw my ascended friends again. Their visits were not usually predictable, although I sometimes got a gut feeling they were coming. They sometimes went months without appearing, giving me time to integrate and practice their words in my everyday life. On this occasion, Pursah began the conversation.

PURSAH: Hello, Gary. How's life treating you?

GARY: Not bad. I had a good time in Lake Charles. They were so grateful to me for coming there! They don't get too many speakers. Everybody goes to Houston or New Orleans—although I had to check out the French Quarter there. It's kind of sad in New Orleans since Katrina. So many people have left. Of course, Bourbon Street, the part of the city that everyone assumed would be destroyed by God, wasn't even touched by the floodwaters. The French were smart enough to build 20 feet above sea level. Anyway, I got to see it and go to a good restaurant, even though there wasn't much time.

And Montreal was fantastic. I really enjoyed going to old Montreal and sampling the food. And my French publisher, Marc, took us to this great Middle Eastern restaurant after the workshop. The dancers were wonderful, and a lot of us from the crowd got up at the end and danced and chanted in a language I didn't understand . . . but it was fun!

PURSAH: As the illusion of time marches on, we're going to get into your personal relationships more. In connection with that, we've got something a little different in store for you today. How would you like to talk to Saint Thomas?

GARY: Excuse me?

PURSAH: Didymus Thomas, Thomas the twin, is available to appear to you right here and talk to you now. You'll see him exactly the way he looked at the age he was at the time of the Crucifixion. He'll speak to you in English instead of Aramaic so you can understand him. He'll look like J did. As you know, Thomas was often mistaken for J because they looked so much alike.

GARY: Yeah! I've had memories and dreams about them, and they looked the same.

ARTEN: Well, now you're going to see him in the flesh, so to speak. Ask him anything you'd like. And remember, there's nothing to be nervous about or intimidated by. You're just talking to yourself. You were Thomas, and you'll be Pursah. They both love you, and all you have to do is be yourself and love them.

GARY: I've been trying to love Pursah for years. But cool. Bring on the dude.

NOTE: Once in a while, my teachers would completely blow my mind. But this was something else. At that instant, Arten disappeared and Pursah morphed into a totally different person. I immediately recognized this person as a man I've seen in my visions. The guy looked very much like—although not exactly—how I remember J looking. J's name was Y'shua at the time. Most people today put the emphasis on the first syllable of that name, but the emphasis should actually be on the second. Of course my teachers just called him J, but this man I was looking at now wasn't J—he was Thomas, or Didymus, the twin, who could easily be mistaken for J. I was dumbstruck and sat in rapt attention as he began to speak.

THOMAS: Hello, brother. You look like you've seen a ghost.

GARY: I don't believe it. Okay, I do. Nothing surprises me anymore, but this is incredible. You look the same way that I've seen you and J look in my dreams and visions.

THOMAS: What did you expect, an imposter?

GARY: No, I didn't mean it like that. Tell me one thing up front. Where did you come from? I've always been a little hazy about that, even with Arten and Pursah.

THOMAS: You saw Pursah change into me. Look at it this way: I'm not appearing to you from the past anymore than Pursah is appearing to you from the future. I'm appearing to you from outside of the system entirely, from completely outside of time and space. I'm a manifestation of the Holy Spirit now. Pursah became enlightened in the future, about a hundred years from now. When you become enlightened and you lay your body aside for the final time, then you are no different from God or J or the Holy Spirit. On the level of spirit, it's all the same. Distinctions are only meaningful in illusions, but there are no illusions in Heaven.

GARY: Then how do you show up here, if you don't recognize illusions?

THOMAS: That's an excellent question. Technically, the answer is that I, Thomas, am not showing up here.

GARY: Come on, will ya? I'm looking at you right now.

THOMAS: Actually, what you're looking at is the Holy Spirit showing up in your dream in a way that you can accept and understand. The Holy Spirit does recognize your illusions, but without believing in them. And the Holy Spirit appears to you in a way that will work the best for you at that time. The Holy Spirit is love, perfect love, just like God. But the love shows up for you as a form, because that's the only way you'd ever be able to hear it. Do you remember what you, Arten, and Pursah once talked about regarding the Holy Spirit's reality?

GARY: Sure. They quoted that *Course* quote: "His is the Voice for God, and has therefore taken form. This form is not His reality. . . ."[2]

THOMAS: Yes, and the Holy Spirit's *reality* is spirit, which is love, real love, all-encompassing.

GARY: So which are you, love or Thomas?

THOMAS: Love. Anyone who has made their transition, enlightened or not, can show up in the dream as a manifestation of the Holy Spirit. But when you do, it's not you—it's an image of you. Once your body passes on, you're out of here, and you never come back as that particular form, unless it's for a review of that lifetime.

GARY: A review?

THOMAS: Yes. It's possible to come back and repeat the same lifetime again. If you learn your lessons better than before, you may even be able to change dimensions of time and experience a different outcome. As Arten and Pursah have said, it's not that you're changing the script, you're just able to view a different dimension of it than you did before.

GARY: I'm familiar with that experience, although you don't usually know you've changed dimensions of time when it happens. It just feels different, like some circumstance has been altered, or maybe some person you know has changed. Maybe things just seem easier.

Say, I want to talk to you about life with J 2,000 years ago, but I want to ask you something else first. I've heard of splits—when there's more than one person who has memories of being a certain person in a previous lifetime.

THOMAS: Right. It would have to be that way by definition.

GARY: Why?

THOMAS: You remember the concept of the mind being like cells dividing under a microscope?

GARY: Sure. It just keeps dividing over and over again. So you start off with two people, like the mythical Adam and Eve, and then 5,000 years later, you've got six billion people. The only way reincarnation would appear to be possible would be if the one being that thinks it's here kept dividing. Then each seemingly separate mind, which many people would call a soul, appears to manifest in the world or the universe as some kind of a body. It could be a human body, but it doesn't have to be. A body is a body. Anything that has a border or a limit—even a piano—is a body. Mind is mind appearing as a symbolic form through the device of separation, and the projection of that separation thought.

THOMAS: Very good. But think for a minute. If the mind keeps splitting, then somewhere down the road you're going to end up with several people who split off from the same apparently individual separate mind! That means they're also going to have the same memories from past lifetimes as the other people who used to be that mind. Of course, this is a linear model, which is illusory. It really happened all at once, and then it looks and feels like you're doing it now. In the linear model, people will have legitimate memories of being the same person.

GARY: So if one person said they were Saint Paul 2,000 years ago and could remember that incarnation, and another person said the same thing, it's possible they could *both* be telling the truth?

Mind is mind appearing as a symbolic form.

THOMAS: Yes, absolutely. And that applies to you as well. There's more than one person walking this planet today who was Saint Thomas 2,000 years ago and would, at times, have legitimate memories of being so.

GARY: That's weird, knowing there's someone else out there who has the same memories as I do in their unconscious mind because we once had the same mind!

THOMAS: Spooky idea. Yet you *still* have the same mind. It just doesn't look that way because you're having a dream of separation. So moving along here, what did you want to know about J?

GARY: I'd like to know if my memories, dreams, visions, and stuff are accurate. For example, when I've been in that vision state of mind, I've seen him as being married to Mary Magdalene, and she was beautiful.

NOTE: There were a few readers who thought *The Disappearance of the Universe* was going along with *The Da Vinci Code,* in saying that J and Mary were married. In reality, the first editions of D.U. and TDC were both published at the same time—in the spring of 2003—and could not have mimicked each other.

THOMAS: Mary was a lot more than beautiful. She was enlightened. She was the same as J, and the disciples were jealous of her for many reasons.

GARY: Why?

THOMAS: First of all, he used to kiss her in public, and that was upsetting to some of us. That sort of thing wasn't done much at the time. Second, she was enlightened like J, and we weren't. On top of that, she was a great teacher. I was a scribe and I understood the teachings better than most, but I certainly didn't want to stand up and speak to people. You've had the same reservations about speaking in front of people during this lifetime, but you overcame them through forgiveness. I respect you for that. But Mary wasn't just a good speaker—she was a spiritual genius.

GARY: Are you saying I'm not?

THOMAS: I don't think the term *genius* would apply.

GARY: What, do you think I'm stupid?

THOMAS: No, I'd just say you're doing the best you can with limited resources.

GARY: And I thought Arten was bad.

THOMAS: I'm just having fun with you, brother! Like I said, I respect you.

GARY: Hey! Do you remember the Last Supper?

THOMAS: Actually, yes, I do.

GARY: That was awesome.

THOMAS: What a lot of people don't realize about the Last Supper was that there was a lot of laughter among the disciples that night, as well as from J and Mary. They usually looked like a normal couple. They had no airs or pretenses about them. That famous painting of the Last Supper, although it's not perfect, does a good job of showing them together that night. As for the laughter, look at the Psalm of David. That's been read at a lot of people's funerals even though it doesn't have anything to do with dying. It's a way of living, fearless living. You can learn to laugh at death. Both J and Mary loved that part of the scripture. It says, "Yay, though I walk through the valley of the shadow of death I will fear no evil, for thou art with me." Of course!

During the Crucifixion, one of the Roman soldiers ran a spike through J's wrist. He didn't feel or show any pain. The soldier was indignant. He screamed at J and demanded, "Why don't you feel any pain?" J looked at him calmly and said, "If you have no guilt in your mind, you cannot suffer." The soldier became outraged at his inability to inflict pain on J, and stuck a spear in his side. It didn't do the soldier any good, or have any effect on J.

At one point, with J nailed to the cross and with his blood flowing down, he gazed lovingly over at Mary and she looked at him. As their eyes connected, a gentle smile came on both of their faces. They knew he had overcome death. He wasn't a body in his mind. What he was couldn't be killed by the world. It couldn't even be hurt by the world! The spirit that he really was, which is no different than God, would go on forever. She was experiencing the same thing as J, and there was nothing anyone in the world could do to alter the truth that was within them.

That's the message of the Crucifixion, or as J put it later in the *Course,* "Teach only love, for that is what you are. If you interpret the crucifixion in any other way, you are using it as a weapon for assault rather than as the call for peace for which it was intended."[3]

GARY: So J overcame death, and I remember some of the things you're saying, and I remember them just the way they happened. Then he appeared to us after the Crucifixion. But you're saying that was really the Holy Spirit appearing as an image of J, although it looked and felt just as real as any other body, which is also the way that you and Arten and Pursah have appeared to me, right?

THOMAS. You've got it. And I have something else for you to consider.

GARY: I'm always open to suggestions. I don't listen to them, but I'm always open to them.

THOMAS: Picture this. J was crucified. We were wanted by the Romans. Most of us, especially Peter, were demoralized. Even

Thaddaeus and I were very challenged. We understood the message of J, as did Mary, Phillip, Stephen, and a few others; but this was still an extremely hard time for most of us. Did we have faith? Did J really overcome death? Certainly none of us was in a frame of mind to go out and claim to the people that he did.

This is where you need to put two and two together. There's *no way* that all the disciples would have gone out into the world and attempted to teach the meaning of what J was saying except for one fact: He *really did* appear to us as a body, just as real, or unreal, as anyone else's body, after the Crucifixion. Anyone who doubts that J overcame death needs to consider that point carefully. How else can you explain the behavior of the disciples unless J actually was resurrected? There would be no logical explanation for our transformed enthusiasm. Yes, his teachings and example before he died were extraordinary and inspiring, but the Holy Spirit knew we were ready for a demonstration to encourage us. Sometimes the Holy Spirit will work with you in a way that will encourage you to keep going on your path. We got the encouragement that we needed.

Eventually, the world would change J's message from a spiritual one to a religious one. But that didn't matter to us at the time. There was no such thing as Christianity. We understood and believed that J had returned to God.

GARY: But you were portrayed as the doubting one.

THOMAS: That was a bunch of nonsense. Just because you want to touch someone who is appearing to you from another worldly realm, it doesn't mean you lack faith. Curiosity alone would be enough of a reason to want to do that. Didn't you want to touch Pursah?

GARY: Yeah, although I probably had more than one reason.

THOMAS: The church made up some things about me; and while they were at it, they completely wrote Mary out of history, rendered the role of Stephen to one of little significance, and said practically nothing about Thaddaeus. They couldn't write me out of history because I was much too well known. I had traveled to many other countries, and a lot of people were aware at the time that I was killed in Chennai, India, which is also called Madras, by a rather confused tribal chief. Incidentally, the place where I got snuffed is now the sight of the Cathedral of San Thome, as it's called there.

GARY: Is it true your bones are there?

THOMAS: Yes, but that's not me, so don't make a big thing out of it. What's important are the teachings.

GARY: Well, speaking of teachings, can you give me an example of how J was teaching the same thing 2,000 years ago as he is today as the Voice of *A Course in Miracles?*

THOMAS: Sure. Look at the response he gave, even in the New Testament, to the elder teachers who asked him, "What is the greatest of the Commandments?" I was there at the time. His answer was incredible. He ignored the elder teacher's beliefs and their scripture. He didn't even acknowledge the Laws of Moses. Instead, he gave them two new Commandments, which were meant to replace the old ones!

GARY: He had big ones.

THOMAS: He had the truth. He said, "On these two Commandments hang all the law and the prophets. You shall love the Lord your God, with all your heart, all your soul and all your mind." And he added, "You shall love your neighbor as you love yourself."

GARY: That reminds me of something. Thomas Jefferson did his own edit of the Bible, now called *The Jefferson Bible*, which Arten and Pursah mentioned to me a long time ago. It wasn't widely available at the time, but it is now. In his own edit, Jefferson also ignored the old scripture completely, including the Laws of Moses. The parts he left in were about how to look at the world and life. That's exactly the same thing that J did in his answer to the teachers!

> **J was about life, real life, which is the love of God.**

THOMAS: Pretty interesting, isn't it? J was about life, real life, which is the love of God. That life is alive, which is why he also said to the teachers, "God is not the God of the dead, but of the living."

There is no real life except in God, Gary. That life, which you will experience permanently in Heaven after you attain enlightenment, is eternal life, which has no opposite. You can experience real life at times even while you appear to be here in a body. But eventually you'll return to life on a permanent basis through true forgiveness, which enables you to undo your ego and go home to God. Any spirituality that doesn't teach you how to do that is going to take a long, long time. But if you undo the ego, you'll know that the seeming opposite to life is death, but death is just a belief that plays itself out in illusions.

You have to understand that the Gospel of Thomas was just a sample of some of the things I wrote down that J said. You already know the version that was discovered in Nag Hammadi wasn't the original. Things were added to it over a period of 300 years. That's why Pursah gave the correct version of the Gospel in your second book, leaving out 44 of the corrupted sayings, plus editing some of the other quotes and even putting a couple of them together. Pursah's version makes much more sense than the Nag Hammadi version because it's consistent, where the other version directly contradicts itself at times. With the consistent version, you can see that his teachings haven't changed. You start to see the Voice of *A Course in Miracles* as it taught our culture 2,000 years ago.

Most of the things I wrote down that J said were eventually destroyed by the church. But there are sayings in other Gospels that J said. Once you learn the *Course,* you can tell for yourself which ones are his and which ones aren't. The more you have Spirit in your mind, the more you can tell what comes from Spirit and what comes from the ego.

I want to give you a couple of the biggest forgiveness lessons I learned in that lifetime. Most lifetimes have a couple of tough ones. Even once you learn there is no order of difficulty in miracles, they're still tough. People shouldn't pretend they're immune to their feelings. Experience your feelings and practice forgiveness. In time the feeling will be one of peace.

One of the hardest lessons for me was the situation that came about because I fell in love with a beautiful and intelligent woman named Isaah. We were perfect for each other on the level of form except for one thing: she was an Arab. A relationship between a Jewish man and an Arab woman at that place and time was culturally taboo. I married her anyway.

Being with her was a joy. She was an excellent belly dancer, and she used to seduce me with it. Part of the reason you're into that sort of thing now is because you're remembering it from that lifetime. She had a good sense of humor, which is an excellent indicator of spiritual advancement. She didn't have any close relatives who were still alive so our marriage wasn't a big problem on her end. But from my side, it was significant. I had been welcome in Nazareth, the town of J, Thaddaeus and I. Thaddaeus was my best friend. We both started following J at the same time. When Isaah came along she really got into his teachings, too. Then she became friends with Mary, whom I already knew, and the five of us would get together once in a while and make merry.

Partly because we got to spend a lot of time with J and Mary and listen to them explain things more, we began to understand what they were teaching on a deeper level than most. Thaddaeus, Isaah, and I felt very fortunate to have each other. It was more than just special relationships. We really understood who the other ones were. So J and Mary could have their special relationship. They could be normal and love each other's bodies. They could go out and have a good time. But at the end of the day they knew who the other really was.

GARY: You're saying that at some point, they'd overlook the body and think of each other as being not just part of it, but all of it—completely innocent and exactly the same as God?

THOMAS: Precisely. And *that's* how they got in touch with their divinity, by seeing it in each other and in everyone else they met. Thaddaeus, Isaah, and I made a great deal of progress toward the goal in that lifetime. We just didn't make it all the way.

Because we were ostracized by the community for being a Jewish-Arab couple, Isaah and I didn't get invited to any weddings. That was a big deal at the time. Weddings were the cultural events of the year. People would travel from hundreds of miles away to see family they hadn't seen in years, and in some cases family members they would be meeting for the first time. By not being invited to any of my relatives' weddings because it meant I would bring Isaah, I was in effect banished from the community and most of my family. That hurt. It was something I eventually forgave after the Crucifixion. I saw what J could go through and still live the teachings, and I could almost see him laughing at me about my situation and saying, "You're feeling bad because of *what?"*

One thing that made my life easier when J was alive was that the five of us—the two couples and Thaddaeus—were close and supported each other a great deal. Plus Phillip and Stephen were close friends. Isaah and I didn't feel like we had no one to talk to because of these friendships.

GARY: Did Thaddaeus ever get married?

THOMAS: I'll let you ask him that. He'll be along soon.

GARY: Oh, God.

THOMAS: You'll be joining God when you're ready, even though in reality you're already there. In fact, you never left. But another forgiveness lesson for me was the way Peter and J's brother James just didn't get it. I always thought they'd come around, but they never did. And I never met Saul, or St. Paul. He came along later when James and Peter had started small churches around the area, including a couple in other countries. James and Peter didn't trust Paul at first, mostly because he had never met J. But when they saw a couple of the letters Paul wrote to the churches and how beautiful and inspirational they were, they changed their minds about him. He was a real crowd pleaser, and the churches loved the suffering and sacrifice angle. Plus James and Peter liked Paul's theology, which was eventually what Christianity was based on, not the teachings of J.

Paul was so articulate he became the leader, the one that early Christians, and later ones, looked up to. But it would be 300 years before the official religion was formed, and Constantine, his wife, and his counsel were the ones who decided what went in their Canon and what was left out. And what was left out got destroyed, which is why most people don't think I was very prolific.

But don't forget, history is just a story. Don't worry about how you look to other people. If you care about how you look, then you're making it real. Why is it always about how it looks? What if it didn't matter what it looks like? Experience your *own* experience, not someone else's.

And forgive anyone who appears to have treated you unfairly. I had to learn that from my relatives scorning me because of Isaah. As a continuum of me, you have to learn it, completely, from those people who tried to ruin you. On the level of form, you're right. You got screwed. What Rev. Larry said was true.

NOTE: When a certain *Course* author (who was the one who instigated the attempts to ruin me) threatened to boycott the 2007 *A Course in Miracles* Conference in San Francisco if I was allowed to speak, one of the sponsors, Rev. Larry Bedini, said to me, "Gary, what they're trying to do to you is wrong."

THOMAS: But this is where you have to be like J. Remember what he says in his most recent teaching, which is the same in meaning, if not always in form, as his teaching 2,000 years ago. He says in the *Course,* "Beware of the temptation to perceive yourself unfairly treated. In this view, you seek to find an innocence that is not Theirs but yours alone, and at the cost of someone else's guilt. Can innocence be purchased by the giving of your guilt to someone else?"[4]

> **If you perceive yourself as unfairly treated, then you're making everything real.**

There's a capital *T* in *Theirs* because what they really are is innocent Spirit, beyond the veil. But if you perceive yourself as unfairly treated, then you're making everything real, which makes the entire ego thought system of guilt real in your mind. The only way to find your innocence is to get that it's *not* real and forgive others for what they have not done in reality. And since it never happened, you can then think of *them* as being innocent. That's the way to have it for yourself. Never forget that. It's the only way out.

I learned it from my family and others. You can learn it from those who project their unconscious guilt onto you. Yes, I had other lessons to learn and so do you, but I made substantial progress and so are you. Hell, you've just got one more time to go!

GARY: Would it be possible for me to forgive so much in this lifetime that I don't have to come back and review that final lifetime as Pursah?

THOMAS: That's a good question, and it shows you want to go home. Technically, it would be possible for you to do that. You have your one remaining power, the free will to choose the true forgiveness of the Holy Spirit instead of the projection of guilt that the ego craves, any time you want. But the Holy Spirit's script of undoing the ego's script calls for you to be here one more time. Remember, you're not going to be the only one who appears to be there. You will be a positive influence on some other people, and that in turn, will help them to practice forgiveness and accelerate their journey home. It's all connected.

GARY: Well, at least I'll get to be a hot babe. That should be interesting.

THOMAS: Whatever you appear to be, don't make it real. Refusing to make it real will keep you on the right track. Don't compromise on the *Course*. You've done a good job; keep it that way.

Christianity put words in J's mouth. In the New Testament, one of the last things they have J saying is, "Father, Father, why hast thou forsaken me?" J would *never* say that. Then if you go back to the old scripture, the Book of Psalms, right at the beginning of Psalm 22 you see the words, "My God, my God, why hast thou forsaken me?" That's a good example of a writer of scripture trying not only to make it look like J is God's only son, but to also take old teachings and superimpose them onto J, trying to build a bridge between Judaism and the budding new religion. Don't buy it.

After the Crucifixion, Thaddaeus, Isaah, and I did a lot of traveling together: Egypt, Syria, Greece, Persia, and eventually India. When we were moving around India, we ran into a warlord who decided to have me executed. He didn't want people from our part of the world, which was the West to him, coming and spreading these crazy ideas of ours.

Now when you get your head cut off, if you have an executioner who really knows what he's doing—his blade is good and sharp, and he hits your neck just right—then when your head comes off, it can live for a minute or two. You can actually see things and think! What do you suppose I was thinking at that time?

GARY: I don't know. How am I gonna get out of this one?

THOMAS: No, I was thinking about J. He had promised me, a couple of years before the Crucifixion, that he'd be there for me when the time came for my transition. He kept his word. He walked up to me, and then I left my body. He guided me to where I was supposed to go next, to the in-between life and along my merry way.

J would be there for anyone. All you have to do is ask. Remember, J and the Holy Spirit are one and the same now, and the *Course* says, ". . . the Holy Spirit will respond fully to your slightest invitation."[5]

Still, being executed was my biggest forgiveness lesson. I knew in the few minutes before it happened that Isaah, who was there, wasn't ready for it. She was distraught and she'd have to watch it, although Thaddaeus, my best friend, turned her head away at just the right time so she didn't see the actual deed.

GARY: Good move. I remember hearing the story, from someone who was there, of how my mother's first husband was killed in a terrible accident. He was on a construction site, which he owned, and there was a wrecking ball that wasn't working right. His pickup truck was parked in its path, and he loved his truck. He ran to it to move it out of the way so it wouldn't be damaged or ruined, and just as he did, the wrecking ball let loose. It took off the top of the truck and his head along with it.

Later, at his funeral, his parents, who were domineering over my mother, insisted on having an open casket. When my mom went to kiss him good-bye, his head fell off. Needless to say, she was traumatized.

THOMAS: Of course. That's an ego special—anything to make the body seem real and have you, your mother, or anyone else react to what happens to it.

I did a pretty good job of forgiving my death when it happened, considering it was such a shocker. I figured the execution was my karma. In India, they have a good way of looking at karma: If it happens to you, that's your karma.

On top of that, I realized later that I had executed that warlord in another dream lifetime. People just keep switching roles. That's why it's best for you to truly forgive those who have trespassed against you. That is what breaks the ego's vicious cycle and frees you from it.

I didn't get to completely forgive the situation with all of my relatives in regard to the way they snubbed and scorned Isaah and me in that lifetime, partly because I was only 36 years old when I got killed. That's why you, as a continuum of me, still have work to do in that area. The form has changed for you. It's not your family that's trying to hurt you now, but a few *Course* authors, which makes it even more ludicrous, but the meaning remains the same. Persevere brother, and knock it out of the park.

I'm going to take off now, but I wanted to give you a little reinforcement about the whole forgiveness thing. It can't be emphasized too much or too often. Most people won't do it in this lifetime. But you don't have to be most people. Be well, my friend. I'll rejoin you in Heaven. Then you'll know that we were never apart.

NOTE: Thomas disappeared instantly, in the same manner as Arten and Pursah's appearances and exits. The second he did, my teachers were both right there in front of me once again.

GARY: Wow! You guys are setting some kind of a record when it comes to messing with my head. I'm sorry—*mind*.

ARTEN: Well, you got a good taste of what it's like to be with one of your past dream incarnations. Why don't we give you a chance to talk with the person I was at that time?

GARY: Thomas said this would happen, but I didn't know it would be today. Give me a break!

NOTE: Arten immediately morphed into a totally different person. Pursah disappeared at the same time, and I instantly recognized the man who was there in Arten's place as another person I've seen in my visions. He was a little overweight and had a beard and long black hair. He was wearing a tunic and looked the way I remembered people looked at that place and time. Thomas had been dressed in the same way, but I had barely noticed it, being mesmerized by the sight of his face. This new visitor was smiling and seemed light and breezy, less serious than Thomas.

THADDAEUS: Remember me, my friend?

GARY: I sure do. Long time no see. I take it you're here to help me along the path, just like Thomas was?

THADDAEUS: It gives me something to do on my day off. Thomas described to you a couple of his most important trials, or lessons, at the time of J. I'll do the same because it helps you put things in perspective. Just as the new scripture teaches you: "Trials are but lessons that you failed to learn presented once again, so where you made a faulty choice before you now can make a better one, and thus escape all pain that what you chose before has brought to you."[6] That applies not only to your current lifetime, but also from one lifetime to another.

GARY: Cool. I'm always happy to find out what I haven't learned.

THADDAEUS: I learned eventually, and you'll learn your lessons, too. You've already learned most of them. Like many advanced spiritual students, you have one or two big ones that you have to make better choices with.

GARY: So what were the big ones during your disciple years or after the Crucifixion?

THADDAEUS: First, you asked Thomas if I was married. Actually, I was gay, and I didn't feel guilty about it. I was as gay as a picnic basket, and proud of it. There were just a couple of problems. For one thing, I was a rabbi; in fact, I was a cantor, which means that I could sing. And I would sing at the Temple. I was good. People liked me, and women were waiting in line to marry me. Not that I was interested in that sort of thing.

So there I was, the singing rabbi—kind of like that person who was popular when you were a kid, the singing nun—and people expected me to be a good rabbi and get married and go forth and multiply. That's what rabbis did, including J, except for the multiply part. And that wasn't the only problem. As a rabbi, I taught the scriptures, God's laws. And what was one of the laws? You remember that little gem from Leviticus, right?

GARY: That all wizards, adulterers, mediums, and homosexuals should be put to death?

THADDAEUS: Nice, huh? So even though I didn't have a problem with being gay, I did have a problem with being dead. It was a phobia of mine. That was a big lesson for me. It wasn't easy to forgive being good at what I did and yet knowing that if I was found out then not only would my life be torn apart, it would be over.

GARY: That's a tough one all right. So what Thomas said about the five of you being friends and really supporting each other, I take it that it helped you get through the difficult times?

THADDAEUS: Absolutely. And one of the things J taught me was that even if my friends weren't around, I was never alone. The Holy Spirit was always with me. Most people think they're alone if they're the only one in the room. But J taught me better.

And he taught me how to forgive, coming from a place of cause and not effect. That's another thing that can't be emphasized often enough. You can't forgive people because they did it. That's what the *Course* calls "Forgiveness to destroy."[7] Forgiving that way is a waste of time. Yet even though 99 percent of *Course* teachers tell people to forgive, they don't teach people the kind of forgiveness that works. It doesn't undo the ego. They make what is being forgiven real. They don't have the gonads to tell people the world isn't real. But, as the *Course* is trying to teach them, because of the way that the mind works, when you make what you're forgiving real, you do *not* free yourself.

When you make what you're forgiving real, you do *not* free yourself.

You tell your own unconscious mind that *you* are guilty! Anyone who does the *Course* and does not understand that and live it is costing themselves a great deal of time, and so are the ones who teach them that way.

The other huge lesson I had to go through and forgive was watching my best friend being executed, which as you know is simply legal murder. The warlord who did it told me to go home to my land and tell people what happens to those who come to his country and try to teach our evil beliefs. I would have felt better if I was executed. But Isaah was there, and I did my best to comfort her. Then, two nights after Thomas was done in, he came to Isaah in her sleep and spoke to her. She told me that it was just as real as anything she had ever experienced. She could touch and feel him. Thomas told her he was fine, and that she would be, too. She wasn't the same after that. It was far more comforting to her than I could ever be.

GARY: Boy, the adventures you guys had. It makes for quite a story, even if the metaphysical aspects of it are a little strange for some people.

THADDAEUS: Truth is stranger than fiction.

GARY: Yeah, I noticed.

THADDAEUS: So before the Crucifixion, we'd travel with J. Isaah was usually with us. Mary was most of the time, although sometimes she'd be off teaching on her own. She had a following, mostly women. She was as good as J in her own way. After J's transition she stayed in Nazareth for a couple of years. Then she went to the south of France where she lived out her life. She didn't have a child like some believe. She taught people and became a living example of enlightenment, or as the *Course* calls it, salvation.

Both J and Mary used metaphors to teach, and J does the same in the *Course*. There are some individuals who teach that everything J said 2,000 years ago—and also those who teach that everything J says in the *Course*—should be taken literally. That's completely *absurd*. When it comes to what J says, the nondualistic truth *should* be taken literally, but *anything* else is a metaphor. If you understand that—2,000 years ago or today—J makes sense. His *Course* makes sense all the way through, and the sayings he really said 2,000 years ago that survived also make sense. And if you *don't* understand that, the *Course* appears to be contradicting itself. There are people who have given up on it because they thought it was contradicting itself when it wasn't. That's just one of many reasons why it's important that teachers know what they're talking about.

GARY: I take it that back in the old days, you guys were taken care of by the people who came to listen to J? Did they give you food and shelter along the way?

THADDAEUS: Most of the time. J's reputation preceded him. Then there were other times when we ended up hungry.

GARY: Did J accept any money?

THADDAEUS: Yes. He worked for tips.

GARY: Seriously.

THADDAEUS: Don't take any of this seriously. You have a sense of humor that's worth keeping. By the way, I didn't talk about the anxiety I had. You'll hear more about that later. . . .

I'm going to take a little nonspatial hike, but I wanted to make an appearance and encourage you. Keep up the good work, and I'll see you around.

NOTE: Thaddaeus disappeared unceremoniously, and my two longtime friends were back—Arten sitting right where Thaddaeus had been and Pursah beside him.

ARTEN: So that's who I was 2,000 years ago.

GARY: That was a real trip. You've given me a lot of trips lately.

PURSAH: Yes, and since you've been visited by your friend Thaddaeus, and yourself, Thomas, from the old days, we're going to tell you a little secret that relates to that time and place.

GARY: If you tell me, it won't be a secret for long.

PURSAH: That's okay. Do you remember the last visit of the first series? We told you that Arten and Pursah were not our real names—that we were using assumed names to stop people from trying to find us in the future?

GARY: Of course I remember.

PURSAH: Well, 2,000 years ago, Arten and Pursah were the names of two friends of ours we would see once in a great while when we traveled to Persia. They were constant figures at an oasis we would stop at on the way. They were friends of J's, too. They met him in the early days, even before I met him.

GARY: Cool; your names aren't random—they were real people, or as real as anyone, and they were friends of yours. You paid tribute to them by using their names.

PURSAH: Yes, they were good people. Of course, we had duality back then, too. You could be robbed and murdered by bandits, or you could be taken in by strangers who became your friends. That's the way of a dualistic world.

GARY: I'm getting pretty tired of duality. It's a drag.

ARTEN: Is that why you drink?

GARY: I think so. I mean, I just don't feel like I belong here.

ARTEN: You don't, but you also know there are better ways to escape from here—just something to think about. We're not going to lecture you, and we're certainly not going to judge you. But in the illusion of time, you're not getting any younger. That's one of the reasons we talked about health.

GARY: I understand. You know Benjamin Franklin said that "health is the first wealth." After seeing what my parents went through, I believe it. I'll start taking better care of myself. Promise.

ARTEN: Very good. That's your decision to make, not ours. And your actions will follow from your decision.

PURSAH: Another thing that would help you would be to stop being concerned about what people think. Don't forget when J said, "Forgive them Father, they know not what they do," the reason they didn't know what they were doing was because they were projecting their unconscious guilt onto him. But they didn't know it. They just thought they were right. Of course, what they really were was insane.

GARY: Not that they were really there.

PURSAH: See, you're getting it. You made their images, but they're not really there. As the *Course* teaches, they are part of the world you made as a substitute reality:

> You who believe that God is fear made but one substitution. It has taken many forms, because it was the substitution of illusion for truth; of fragmentation for wholeness. It has become so splintered and subdivided and divided again, over and over, that it is now almost impossible to perceive it once was one, and still is what it was.

That one error, which brought truth to illusion, infinity to time, and life to death, was all you ever made. Your whole world rests upon it. Everything you see reflects it, and every special relationship that you have ever made is part of it [8]

And now you know the way out, Gary. You use the mind to choose between the body and spirit, and which one you make a habit of choosing will become real for you. As J puts it, the mind is "the activating agent of spirit. . . ."[9]

ARTEN: You're not here, buddy. And you'll experience that even more now. You deserve it. Your forgiveness has served you well, and will continue to do so. We'll see you next time. Until then, remember these words from the *Course,* and be assured that your salvation is secure:

Forgiveness is the key to happiness. I will awaken from the dream that I am mortal, fallible and full of sin, and know I am the perfect Son of God.[10]

6

LESSONS OF GARY

As you condemn only yourself, so do you forgive only yourself.[1]

By June of 2007, Karen and I had both made decisions. We knew it was time to go our separate ways. We each hired a lawyer, and the process of divorce had begun. It was a trying time for both of us. We'd been together for 26 years, 25 of them married. It's not like we didn't try.

It was 20 years before that, in August of 1987, that I had made another decision. It was the Harmonic Convergence, where the planets of our solar system aligned, and millions of people around the globe stood in their circle of truth and made statements of what their beliefs and intentions were. After that, many lives started to go in different directions. It was all connected, as it must be. For me, after eight years of playing with my band, Hush, mostly in the Boston area, and sometimes around New England, I decided I wanted to change my life.

Although Beverly, Massachusetts, and Poland Spring, Maine, are only two and a half hours apart, they are two different worlds. A suburb of Boston, the Beverly-Salem area is densely populated, and if you want to, it's easy to find life in the fast lane. You can get to downtown Boston in 40 minutes. I must have gone to Fenway Park a hundred times; partied in nightclubs in Kenmore Square if the game got out early enough; and to aid my spiritual life, frequented the est center on Newbury Street for years.

Poland Spring is a small town about 45 minutes north of Portland and 45 minutes south of Augusta, the state capital. Spread out over several rural miles, it's a very quiet and laid-back place. There are no sidewalks or streetlights. In the winter the temperature is often 10 degrees below Boston's temperature and 20 degrees below New York City's. If it's raining in Boston, it will probably be snowing in Maine, at least from Portland on up. This is country living, and I was a city boy. Culture shock was something I would encounter firsthand. Good comedies have been made about the same predicament, but after a while, for me, it wasn't funny.

"Est" was a transformative program created by Werner Erhard in 1974. I did the est training, as it was called, at the Ramada Inn near Logan International Airport in December of 1978. After suffering from debilitating depression for seven years, and mild depression another seven years before that, est was just what I needed. It gave me my first thought system. That in turn provided me with a new and consistent way of thinking about everything I saw, and interpreting it in a way that snapped me out of my depression within two years. Est wasn't *A Course in Miracles,* but it was a very good education for the mind given in an amazingly short time. It was also an excellent training ground for the *Course.* Over a period of nearly 14 years, about a million people did "the training," as its enthusiasts called it. I'd venture to guess that at least 100,000 of them went on to study *A Course in Miracles.*

During that Harmonic Convergence in 1987, a woman named Doris Lora also made a decision. She moved herself and her daughter, Cindy, from Ohio to sunny Southern California. Her other daughter, Jackie, was already in college and ended up joining them in California at a later time. Doris, a brilliant woman with two Ph.D.'s—one in music and one in psychology—had been influenced by Shirley MacLaine, as I was at the time, and felt compelled to start a new life among the free-thinking people of "SoCal."

Doris drove the two of them halfway across the country. When they were driving in Texas, she was exhausted and almost out of gas. She didn't know if she could make it much longer. She called out, "Please tell me. Am I doing the right thing?" Doris got her answer.

Suddenly a force started pushing the car forward. It was like Doris didn't even have to drive for a while. The car was being helped, and the two passengers inside along with it. It was the Holy Spirit empowering the mind to bring Doris and her daughter to where they were supposed to be. Much later I'd find it fascinating that people would simultaneously make decisions halfway across the country from one another that would one day end up bringing them together. At the same time Doris and Cindy were moving, I was in the process of changing directions and going toward Maine, which in turn would one day lead me to the same place these two people were. The *Course* says, "There are no accidents in salvation. Those who are to meet will meet, because together they have the potential for a holy relationship. They are ready for each other."[2]

> **We're destined to one day come back together again in another place and time.**

It's as though groups of us are in each other's orbits, and even though we appear to move apart, we're destined to one day come back together again in another place and time to act out our relationships and have another chance to enjoy the good in them, forgive the negative details of them, and see each other as we really are.

After that decision in 1987, it took me two years to get out of my band because I had my signature on many contracts, and I had the band booked a year and a half in advance. I moved to Maine on January 1, 1990, and would live there for 17 and a half years.

During that time, California wasn't even on my radar. I still dreamed of living in Hawaii. Even in 2004, a year after *The Disappearance of the Universe* had been published, I had never been to California except for one very brief foray. Then I made my first real trip there. I remember my host, Tom, driving me down Ocean Avenue in Santa Monica. I liked what I saw. As I looked around I was thinking, *This is really cool!* After that visit, Pursah, as reported in my second book, asked me, "How'd you like California?" When I told her how much I loved it, she said, "Good. You'll be going there many times. Enjoy." She knew something I didn't.

During that trip I checked into the Hyatt on Sunset Strip, a hotel that has since been replaced by another. I went out for my first walk in Hollywood, having no idea where I was or where I was going except that I was on the famous Sunset Strip, and I was completely starstruck just being there. I've been a huge movie fan my whole life. Now I was where it all happened.

After walking down the street for a while, I wandered into a mall and saw a Virgin Records store. I don't know why I decided to go in but I did, even though a well-known record store isn't representative of Hollywood history. As I walked around, looking at the music selections and the people, I saw a woman standing in one of the aisles. A strong feeling of recognition swept over me.

She was short and thin, with auburn hair and a beautiful face. She glanced at me briefly, but we didn't connect. I stared at her for about a minute. Later I was grateful she was busy looking at a CD and didn't bust me for gawking at her. I felt a strong sensation that I knew her—that this wasn't the first time I was seeing her, even though I knew it wasn't in this lifetime.

It may be hard for people who have seen and heard me speak in public to believe this today, but for almost all of my life, I was incredibly shy. It wasn't like I could just walk across the room and talk to a woman—that wouldn't even be within the realm of possibility. And I didn't go over and talk to this woman, but I would never forget her face. It was implanted in my mind. I'd think of her often, and kick myself for not saying hello. But what would I have said: "I think I've known you before in another lifetime"? That would have sounded like a pretty bad pickup line. Besides, I was married. After a minute, the woman walked away.

Two years later I was speaking in Las Vegas, the spiritual capital of the world. I was doing a conference for my publisher Hay House, and after my presentation I did a book signing. During the signing, a pleasant woman came up to have her book autographed. She was kind and friendly; I guessed she was in her late 60s. I also felt a connection with this woman, although I couldn't quite put my finger on why. She said nice things about my work, and we exchanged pleasantries. The woman was Doris Lora.

Then it happened. The next person in line approached me and started speaking. I couldn't believe who I was looking at. Everything came to me all at once: I knew that this woman was the man I had seen in my visions as Thaddaeus 2,000 years ago. I knew who she was and would be during this lifetime. I knew she would be a man named Arten—one of my ascended-master teachers—a hundred years from now, and I also knew she was the woman I had seen in that record store in Hollywood two years before.

She told me her name, Cindy Lora, and said she was a musician. She had lived in California since 1987, when her mom had driven her out there from Ohio. She knew from *Disappearance* that I was also a musician, and told me she had a website. I couldn't think too clearly as I was a little freaked out, but I tried to stay calm. I couldn't let her get away again. Even if nothing came of it, I at least had to get to know her. I asked her if there was a way to get in contact with her through her website. She said yes, and after a minute, it was time for me to keep signing books. She left with her mom, but she didn't leave my mind.

I communicated with Cindy a couple of times by e-mail. It turned out that she was also married—to a guy named Steve. However, as we got to know each other better, it was apparent to both of us that our marriages were over. Cindy and I didn't see each other very much the first year after we met, but once Karen and I had each filed for divorce, and Cindy filed for divorce from Steve, I asked the Holy Spirit, as I always do, for guidance. The answer was as clear as could be. I asked Cindy to look for an apartment in the L.A. area and move in with me. On June 18, 2007, I flew to California, and was determined to never live any place east of there again.

Every state has its own divorce laws. In Maine, the law says that the divorcing pair should try to work out their own settlement. The idea is to save the court time and money. As part of the process, the two spouses and their attorneys are supposed to have a meeting along with another lawyer who is called the "divorce mediator"—or as I thought of it, the referee. So in August, I was flying off to Maine to meet with Karen and the others in an office in the Lewiston, Maine, courthouse.

I was the last one to walk in the room, and it felt tense. Karen looked nervous, and her lawyer looked angry. The mediator opened the meeting, and after the instructions, the gloves came off. Karen and I were fine, but we couldn't get these two lawyers to agree on anything. It turned out this wasn't the first time the two of them had done this. They had a history, and you could feel the resentment between them, especially on the part of the middle-aged woman who represented Karen. My lawyer was an older gentleman who was rather subdued, like an elder statesman, but Karen's rep was anything but that. After she accused me of going out to $300 lunches (I had once taken several people out on an important business lunch, and paid for it), I asked her how much money she wanted for Karen. Her answer was, "All of it."

That didn't quite seem fair to me. I was willing to split everything 50/50. In a "no fault" state like California, that would be the standard practice. But in Maine, the law states that if you've been married for more than ten years, someone has to pay spousal support, even if there are no children. Since I made the most money, I was elected.

Still, there was no consensus in the room, and the bickering between the lawyers seemed pointless. After two hours, we took a break. Before I arrived in Maine, Karen and I had planned to have dinner together. I reminded her during the break, and she still wanted to go. No progress was made during the meeting, and our mediator suggested that the two sides should continue to try to work out some kind of an arrangement rather than having a judge do it. Karen's lawyer didn't want her to go to dinner with me, but we agreed anyway to meet that night at Applebee's, the finest restaurant in Auburn, Maine.

Karen had gotten into the *Course* for about two years in the 1990s, and we went to the same *A Course in Miracles* study group in Lee, Maine, which is even smaller than Poland Spring. Karen liked, even loved, the people in the study group, but at the time her heart wasn't into it. It was more as though she was doing it because I was, and after a while, she developed her own interests and stopped doing the *Course* and going to the group, except on special occasions like Christmastime.

But when I left, that changed. Karen got back into the *Course*. It was almost like I had to leave for her to do that, it had to be her idea. After a couple of months I was amazed by how deeply she was getting it. She started doing the Workbook again and began studying Ken Wapnick's *Journey Through the Workbook* at the same time. A masterwork, experiencing that book at the same time as the *Course* is like doing the Workbook with Ken. He not only explains the lessons but also correlates many of them with the quotes in the Text that they correspond to. It would take students at least a decade, if not several, to do that on their own. Ken, who knows the *Course* like no other, has done it for them.

Forgiveness can be very practical. When Karen and I sat down for dinner that night, the atmosphere was totally different from the meeting room that afternoon. As soon as we started to talk, it reminded me of the old days when we could go to dinner and enjoy ourselves, not doing anything but just being there. We talked about the good times. We reminisced about our dog, Nupey, who had made her transition about eight years before that, after living with us as a member of the "pack" for 15 years.

Nupey knew her place in the pack. I was the leader, and if Nupey needed protection, or if I did, we would have each other's back. If she heard thunder, which scared her, she'd run and jump in the bathtub. It was my job to reassure her and see her through. Karen was second in the pack, and Nupey considered it her job to protect her. Nupey would look up to me, but if Karen and I ever got into an argument, Nupey would suddenly get in between us as if to protect Karen, not that she needed it. But Nupey sensed that between the two of us, protecting Karen was supposed to be her priority. It was cool to watch the dynamics of it, and it was fun for Karen and me to talk about it that night.

We had both been practicing forgiveness—a lot. That's why there was no animosity at the table that evening. And after awhile, I had what seemed to be an inspired idea. I took a napkin and wrote down a brief, proposed divorce settlement. Then I gently pushed the napkin over to Karen and said, "What do you think about that?" She replied, "I don't know. Why don't you come over tomorrow, and we'll talk about it."

It felt strange going back to the old place. Even though it had only been two months, it felt like two years. I found that the more I did, the more time seemed meaningless. Things I did a month ago felt like they happened a year ago. A year ago felt like three. Here I was, back at the last place I had lived in New England, and it seemed like it was another person who had lived there—not me.

Karen answered the door, and she was friendly. Right away, she handed me a piece of paper. It was an alternative divorce settlement. I looked it over for a minute. There were a couple of details I didn't want, so I changed them a little. I handed the paper back to her, asking, "What do you think of that?" She thought for a minute, and then looked at me and said, "Okay."

The practicality of forgiveness can show itself in many ways, or the effects may not be observable at all.[3] The *Course* says the miracle, which is the kind of forgiveness that comes from a place of cause and not effect, can "produce undreamed of changes in situations of which you are not even aware."[4] If I was driving on the freeway in L.A. and suddenly someone cut me off in traffic, I could forget myself, especially if I wasn't in a very good mood, and give the guy who cut me off the finger. And what if that guy had a gun? I could be dead. If I forgive, I'm alive. That's a very practical and very different outcome. I'm not changing the script; I'm determining dimensions of time without being consciously aware of it. In one dimension of time I remain alive, and in the other I'm a deceased statistic of road rage.

> **I'm determining dimensions of time without being consciously aware of it.**

And in the obscurity of Maine, Karen and I worked out in just a few minutes' worth of talking what it would have taken those two lawyers two years to work out, and they would have gotten a good deal of the money. Later, my lawyer was fine with the agreement. Karen's lawyer wasn't, but Karen stuck to her position. I left the state the next day, but I would have to return in two months.

Even if you work out your own divorce settlement, a judge still has to approve it, and the divorce decree must be filed at the courthouse by the clerk of courts. You never really know what's going to happen when you go to court. Even if you have an agreement, a judge can inflict his opinion on it. And in a court, the judge's opinion is the law, unless it's overturned later.

I returned to Maine in October, and checked into a hotel on the Androscoggin River. Most places in New England, whether they are towns, mountains, or rivers, are named either after a Native America tribe or a town in England. The river, named after a Native American tribe, separated Auburn from Lewiston. After the Indians, Lewiston had been settled by the French, who pushed their way down from Quebec. In fact, Maine had once been a part of Canada. Eventually, it became part of Massachusetts before becoming its own state in 1820.

That night, I took a walk on a path along the river. It was warm for Maine in October, and the fresh air felt good. Then something happened that I never would have expected. In shamanism, the notion of "power animals" is a widely held belief. The idea is that when an animal comes into your space then—depending on what the animal is and especially what its attitude is, friendly or hostile—it represents a premonition of your near-term future, because it's symbolic of the kind of energy you're drawing into your space at that time. I've always been a believer in signs, and I don't ignore them when they present themselves.

As I was walking along the river, I heard the sound of a goose honking. Then I heard a second one. They were behind me. I've heard geese before, flying near the house on White Oak Hill in Poland Spring, but I'd never seen any. Then in an instant the geese were right over me. They couldn't have been more than 50 feet above me. My impression was that they were happy. I'm not sure what happy honking sounds like, but they seemed to be having a good time. Then I was astonished by what they did. The two geese that were flying together all of a sudden turned and flew in exact opposite directions—one straight to my left, and one straight to my right. I couldn't believe it, and the message could not have been clearer.

I knew that the next day the judge would not only approve our divorce settlement, but that it would also turn out to be a good thing. Karen and I were going to fly off in different directions, but we were both going to be happy.

The next morning went smoothly. The judge was a good guy, and he just asked us a few routine questions. "Are you sure this is what you want? Is this what you agreed to? Are you on drugs?" Then we went with the clerk, and she filed the papers so everything was nice and legal. But Karen looked sad. When we were leaving, she said to me, "You got what you wanted, Gary." That brought up feelings of guilt in me. I could see that Karen was still hurting. I didn't realize at the time that the breakup of a long-term relationship sometimes involves going through some of the same grieving stages you endure with the death of a loved one. At first there may be anger and then denial, and other stages that hopefully will lead to acceptance. Even if you've engaged in true forgiveness, any one of those stages can pop up again unexpectedly, until they are completely healed. Karen was expressing her disappointment, and I had to allow it.

That night, although I was relieved the divorce proceedings were over, I was thinking of what Karen had said. I felt like going out and drinking. Then, God bless them, my teachers showed up just when I needed them the most. It would be their shortest visit in history. Arten and Pursah seldom told me anything about my personal future, but in this case they felt it was right to make an exception. I don't know what would have happened that night if they hadn't shown up. But I was very happy that they were suddenly sitting in my hotel room, which conveniently had a couch.

ARTEN: So, it's over. How do you feel?

GARY: Kind of weird. I'm sure you know what Karen said when we were leaving.

PURSAH: Don't worry, Gary. Tomorrow Karen is going to call you, and the two of you will get together tomorrow night. You'll have a bit of a party, and you're going to be friends. Everything is going to be fine. Enjoy.

GARY: Really?

Lessons of Gary

ARTEN: That's it, brother. We're out of here. Be good.

They surprised me coming, and they surprised me going. But I felt better. I watched TV that night and was thinking how amazing it was that my visitors said Karen would call me the next day. Was it true? Yes, it must be. My teachers had earned my trust. The Manual for Teachers in the *Course* teaches development of trust, but it's not some kind of a blind, religious faith. I tell people that the Holy Spirit will earn their trust. It's their experience that will tell them the Holy Spirit is always with them, looking out for their true, best interest. And sometimes a symbol of spirit will show up in the world. If the symbol is truly of the spirit, then the reality behind the symbol can always be trusted, and so can the message that is communicated through the symbol.

Karen called me the next day and asked how long I was in town and if I was busy that night. We had a nice dinner and ended up having drinks in my room. She seemed more relaxed that night than I had seen her in years. It was as though a heavy burden had been lifted from her shoulders. *Me.* We had a good time, and I felt that a new phase had begun in our relationship. It wasn't over— just changing.

Two months later, Karen called me to wish me a Merry Christmas. She also had news. She was moving to Hawaii! After a tinge of jealousy at knowing she would attain the dream of living on the Islands before I did, I felt happy for her. I knew that ever since the first time we had gone there in 1986 she loved Hawaii the same way that I did. She was going to buy a condo in Waikiki. I congratulated her and told her I was surprised, not so much that she would move to Oahu, but that she would leave her mother. Her mom was her best friend, and here was Karen moving over 5,000 miles away. That was a move that took determination and courage. I was impressed.

As for me, I knew I was exactly where I was supposed to be, and meeting exactly the people I was supposed to meet. There was work for me to do in California, maybe even the Hollywood I had been so starstruck by. I didn't know how the script would play itself out, but I had to play my part. I knew there would be challenges—there always were. But, as with all the stages of life, there would be some challenges I didn't expect.

In February, I happened to be in Oahu, doing a Workshop at the Diamond Head Unity Church, which was arranged by my agent, Jan. A few of us took Karen out for dinner on her birthday, February 13. She seemed peaceful and content. At one point, we did a preplanned gag where someone proposed a toast and said, "Raise your glasses!" On cue, we all put on a pair of Marx Brothers' glasses with the phony noses and mustaches. People in the upscale restaurant just stared at us. It was fun to be able to act silly and just not care what anyone thought.

When I left Hawaii and moved through my speaking schedule, I realized I had to admit something. I couldn't write and travel at the same time. There were too many distractions on the road. There was always something to do, from the traveling itself to meeting people, going to lunches and dinners with workshop organizers and readers, preparing for the all-day events and then doing them, getting enough rest to function effectively, trying to keep up with communications . . . it was hectic and challenging. It was also a forgiveness opportunity. I *wanted* to share the message of the *Course* and my books with people. But the people also wanted books, more than anything, and I had already committed myself to a couple more years of continuous travel.

I wanted to talk to my teachers about this and several other important forgiveness lessons that were facing me. For example, even though I thought I had forgiven my relationship with my parents, occasionally memories would pop up in my mind of me not being the kind of a son I would have liked to be, if only I had the capacity to do it at the time. Also, there were still memories of my time in Maine that weren't pleasant, as well as memories of my years as a musician, and some of the people I had worked with. Then there was the huge move I had made to California, and the lifestyle changes and additional culture shock I was going through, plus new relationships to explore.

In late 2009, after I had been living in my new adopted state for two years and four months, I got a letter in the mail from the

Internal Revenue Service. Just when you think you've got enough to forgive, the IRS shows up.

When Karen and I began to physically split up, she started taking money out of the bank accounts, so I figured I should do the same thing. We had three accounts: checking, savings, and ironically, one to set money aside for taxes. So I opened up three more accounts just in my name. Several months later I moved to California and opened up three new bank accounts. Now there were nine. Apparently, this set off a red flag with the IRS, and they decided to audit me—and not just for 2007, but also for 2008. They claimed that the money I moved to California was income. It wasn't. It was money I had earned and already paid taxes on. They didn't seem to care, and what ensued was a process that lasted well into the year 2012 of trying to demonstrate that I didn't owe them any money. It was a very difficult and frustrating two and a half years, and a major distraction from my work.

One of the problems is that when the IRS audits you, the burden of proof is on you. You are guilty until you prove yourself innocent! The fact that the approach is un-American doesn't seem to have any relevance to the matter.

My ascended friends, seeing all of this, but not putting any belief in it, which is how the Holy Spirit's true perception functions, came to me on an afternoon when they knew I had some extra time.

ARTEN: Well, hotshot, you've had your hands full. I know it's frustrating for you because people can't see most of what you do. They just want to know where the damn book is.

GARY: Tell me about it. I'm a little surprised how judgmental some of them are.

PURSAH: Give people a chance to project, and they'll take it! Of course, they don't know that they're projecting; like others we've talked about, *they* just think they're right.

ARTEN: Yes, but your mistake wasn't in not finishing the book yet. The mistake you made was in *telling* people about the book. If they didn't know about it, they wouldn't be upset that it's not available. From now on, maybe you shouldn't tell people about a book until it's complete. Then they'll be pleasantly surprised, instead of getting their bowels in an uproar.

GARY: Yeah, I won't make that mistake again. Now if I can just cut down on the traveling, I'd be able to do a lot more writing.

PURSAH: We *have* counseled you to cut down. Maybe you should listen to us a little more often. In fact, maybe you should listen to yourself a little more often, since you've expressed the intention of staying home more. Instead of just saying something like that, you should follow through on it.

GARY: I know. I bit off more than I could chew. I've got to get better organized and get control of my illusions, like time and stuff.

ARTEN: Then do it my friend. In any case, there *has* been an excellent development that has come from your traveling, speaking, and your practice of forgiveness, aside from the fact that your workshops help so many people for the rest of their lives.

GARY: What's that, oh tall, dark, and handsome one?

ARTEN: Save the flattery for Pursah. The excellent development is that you've overcome your shyness. Do you remember the first time you went out to do a workshop?

GARY: Yeah. I was so scared I didn't think I could make it. If I didn't remember the Holy Spirit when I got out there, I don't think I *would* have made it. Of course, after that I figured out that I should join with the Holy Spirit before I went onstage. And I've learned how to practice forgiveness on the audience. Instead of thinking of them as really being there, which would put me at the effect of what I'm seeing, I visualize them as coming from me. Now I'm at cause, and they're not really there. It's a projection that's coming from the unconscious, the big part of the mind people can't see.

The American Indians used to say, "Behold the great mystery." Well, the *Course* says, "Behold the great projection,"[5] because that's all it is. It's just one great big mother freakin' projection that we've bought into. It doesn't exist. There *is* no universe of time and space; there's only a projection of a universe of time and space! Thinking of it in that way, I can overlook the images I'm seeing and look to the truth of spirit that's beyond the veil. *That's* spiritual sight. It's also the third step in forgiveness. With spiritual sight there's only the truth, so there's nothing to fear. I love what the Course says about miracles, "They heal because they deny body-identification and affirm spirit-identification."[6] That's really cool.

There *is* no universe of time and space; there's only a projection of a universe of time and space!

PURSAH: How comprehensive. You keep getting it more deeply all the time. And we really want to emphasize that third step, because very few are doing it, and almost none of the teachers are stressing it. Yet without it, forgiveness is not accomplished. It's not whole until you think and see in terms of wholeness, the way the Holy Spirit does.

So, you were as nervous as a kitten that first time out. And today you walk into a place like you own it. Speaking to a group of people for you is no longer stressful. It's like brushing your teeth. And that's the way it should be. In fact, nothing should be any more stressful than brushing your teeth. Congratulations on your excellent progress in that area.

ARTEN: Have you been able to walk across a room and talk to a beautiful woman?

GARY: I'm sure I could at this point, but I don't have to.

ARTEN: Yes. We'll talk about your new relationship later.

PURSAH: So let's complete your old relationships. You've almost completely forgiven your relationship with your parents. You thought you were a bad son because you couldn't help them when they needed you, but you've learned since then, through your personal mystical experiences, that they've forgiven you. So what's the problem? Maybe the problem is that the person you really need to forgive is yourself. We'll come back to that.

Your memory, which at times is a blessing because you have such a good one, and it helps you remember the Course, can also be a curse. You remember the bad times. That's what the ego wants, because it makes the whole thing real.

GARY: Yeah. A long time ago I heard the actress Ingrid Bergman say that the secret to happiness is good health and a bad memory. If you had a bad memory, you wouldn't be thinking about the bad times and the things people did to you.

PURSAH: Yes, that's true. But in your case, when a past memory comes up that makes you feel bad, you should remember what the *Course* says it's for. It's for forgiveness, just like any other negative thing. Whether what's in your mind is from the past, present, or future doesn't matter. It's all the same because it's all equally untrue. Having bad memories is actually one form of what the *Course* calls mind wandering. Remember, it says, "You are much too tolerant of mind wandering, and are passively condoning your mind's miscreations."[7] The ego loves mind wandering, and bad memories are a great way to keep you stuck in your bodily identification, because the feelings that come along with the bad memories make you think that it's all true, which means everything you remember happening really happened. That in turn, makes *all* of it real. But the Holy Spirit is telling you that *none* of it is real!

GARY: So how do I forgive the past?

PURSAH: The same way you forgive what's right in front of your face now. What is a memory, except a picture in your mind? And what's this that you're seeing right now, except a picture in your mind? So when you catch yourself passively condoning your mind's miscreations, you need to take charge. Stop thinking with the ego, switch to the Holy Spirit, and stop making it real.

GARY: Right. Like sometimes I have memories from being in my last band throughout the '80s, and before that, too, all the way back to 1965—and there are a lot of good memories, but also hurtful ones. I still remember a lot of the rude, even obnoxious things a couple of people in the band said to me. I remember one drummer was a real asshole.

ARTEN: You just made it real.

GARY: I'm sorry. I meant, I remember this one dream figure that was an image I projected from my own unconscious mind who was a scapegoat for my guilt over the original separation from God, who occasionally appeared to say things to me that one might consider to be inappropriate.

ARTEN: Lengthy but accurate. By the way, don't ever say you're sorry. It implies guilt.

GARY: Anyway, I tried to be good to this guy, and I championed him for a while, but he was a constant troublemaker, and I ended up hating him. I remember he would get bad allergies in the spring—terrible hay fever. I liked that. I used to enjoy his suffering. It was like vicarious revenge.

ARTEN: And?

GARY: Even recently, I'd have memories of some of the things he said to me and start to feel activated. I've forgiven most of those times, but it's like you have to be on the lookout for memories that bother you because they seem to come out of nowhere, and they can come at any time. I guess it doesn't matter what they are. The ego will keep throwing things at you, and most of the time it appears to be from the outside, even though it's really from the inside—although I guess ultimately it's all the same, because none of it's true.

PURSAH: That's why perseverance is the most important quality a *Course* student can have. When the *Course* says, "Be vigilant only for God and His Kingdom,"[8] it's not just blowing smoke.

GARY: Yeah, I guess when I decided all those years ago that I wanted to remove conflict from my life, I didn't realize what a tall order it was.

PURSAH: Yes, be careful what you ask for. But you would have had to go through the undoing of your ego eventually, so why not do it sooner rather than later? The later you do it, the more you prolong your suffering.

GARY: So it seems that no matter what it is, it's all the same. Like moving all the way across the country, going through even more culture shock, experiencing new relationships, most of them cool but some of them weird . . . it is all one big forgiveness opportunity.

ARTEN: Yes, but remember, it's the little everyday things you forgive that add up to salvation. By practicing forgiveness on those everyday things—not getting what you want, for example—your mind gets into the habit of forgiveness. Then, when something that appears to be really big happens that you need to forgive, you'll be much more likely to be able to do it because your mind has been trained to forgive. I'm not saying it will be easy to forgive those seemingly *big* things, but you've made it much more possible because of your practice, even if it takes you awhile to forgive them.

Then on occasion you have comic relief, and the good times that you should also remember. When you think of the past, think of when a person was expressing love. That in turn helps keep you in a loving frame of mind. Remember all the times you've laughed. Laughter is definitely of the Holy Spirit, as long as it's not at someone else's expense. Laughter helps you feel and experience that this world cannot be taken seriously. It's too crazy! It's worthy of laughter, not tears. Tears make it real and keep you stuck here.

GARY: But what about people who go through tragedies. Certainly you don't expect them to laugh.

ARTEN: Not at the time. That's when you should remember Ken's advice: "Don't forget how to be normal." Let them grieve. Let them have their experience. Even-

> **Instead of seeing people as victims, think of them as what they truly are.**

tually they'll be able to forgive the tragedy, when they're ready. In the meantime, it's *your* job to forgive, and instead of seeing people as victims, think of them as what they truly are, which is perfect spirit.

PURSAH: When it comes to the good times, tell us one of your funny experiences on the road.

GARY: Okay. I was speaking in Washington State, in a suburb of Seattle, and this nice girl named Shelora was supposed to drive me to the workshop. So she picked me up, and she had a lot of questions she wanted to ask, so we got to talking. She found the highway we were supposed to be on, and we were traveling along and talking quite a bit, maybe half an hour, because she kept asking questions.

Then to her horror, we suddenly crossed the border into Canada! She had been going the wrong way! Yes, she was on the right highway, but she went north instead of south. Now we were in trouble, and for more than one reason. First, even if we could get going back in the right direction, we'd be at least an hour late for the workshop. Second, we could see the other side of the road and the line of cars that was waiting to get into the U.S. It looked like it might take three hours to go through the whole line. That would make us four hours late for the workshop, probably canceling it. Third, and possibly more important, we'd have to explain what we were doing in Canada. This was 2005, just before you had to have a passport to go between Canada and the U.S. You used to be able to use a birth certificate. Of course that day we didn't have birth certificates on us either, just driver's licenses. So, what the hell could we do?

Practice forgiveness, which we did. We forgave the whole situation. We didn't make it real. We forgave and asked for the Holy Spirit's guidance. Then Shelora saw a small connector between the two roads. She took it, and begged the driver who was in one of the cars heading south to please let her cut into the line. This was a hell of a long line, and that person had certainly been waiting for a long time. We couldn't have blamed the driver if she wouldn't let us in. Shelora held her hands up as if in prayer to the person. The driver of that car, seeing that Shelora was praying for help, let her cut into the line. Ten minutes later we were at the border crossing.

I think the guard saw us cross the border and go into Canada and turn around to go back. The Canadian checkpoint was a little farther in, so we hadn't gotten that far yet. Shelora was wise enough to tell the truth, and admit she didn't realize she was going the wrong way and had crossed the border accidentally. The guard could see she was sincere and that her story matched what he had seen. He let us go back into the U.S. and didn't even ask for an I.D.! I don't know if they would be that lenient today. It seems that America has gotten stricter every single year since then. You know, give them an inch and they'll take a mile. But on this lucky day, we practiced forgiveness, did what we were guided to do, and we were back in the States!

With that behind us, we figured we'd be an hour to an hour and a half late. About a half hour later, I really had to go to the bathroom and we spotted a rest area. We pulled over and I went in. When I tried to go to the bathroom, I pulled down my zipper and it broke! That had never happened to me before. So now I was walking around with my fly undone because the zipper was broken.

Then we got to the workshop, and the two of us walked in together. There was a nice guy in the audience whom the workshop organizer had asked to sing and play his guitar as a warm-up that morning. He played longer than expected, and helped keep the people happy until I got there. Then I walked up to speak and told the crowd, "I'm sorry that Shelora and I are late, and the fact that my zipper is broken has absolutely nothing to do with our tardiness."

PURSAH: Good story. And it got a good laugh.

GARY: Yes, and sometimes I don't want to joke and laugh, like with this whole IRS thing. I'm doing my best to forgive this one, but it's a real pain in the ass. No matter how much information you give them, they want more. It never ends.

PURSAH: For you, you're going through what I called a slow burn during the first series of visits to describe what I went through with the student who hurt my career in my final lifetime. A slow burn is always one of your biggest forgiveness lessons. You're going to have to be particularly determined with this one.

One good thing is that you're being practical on the level of form. You asked for guidance, and that led you to someone who referred you to a good CPA, and you're letting her help you. She knows that you can't be intimidated by the IRS, and they *will* try to intimidate you. They'll try to get you to pay money you don't owe. They don't always follow the law, and sometimes they don't even follow their own guidelines. Their goal is to get money from you, and a lot of people are so intimidated they'll pay it even if they shouldn't have to.

The IRS knows that most people won't take them to court. Most would rather pay, if they can, and get the whole thing over with. What they don't know is that when the IRS goes to court, they lose 80 percent of the time. That's because they don't follow the law. During the auditing process, the burden of proof is on you, which is wrong, but that's the way it is. If you go to court, however, now the burden of proof is on them. They have to prove their case, and most of the time they can't. But they're hoping you won't go through the expense of hiring a tax lawyer. They know even if you win you'll sometimes end up paying the tax lawyer as much as you would have had to pay them. The system is obviously rigged in their favor.

We're not going to get into the fact that the IRS was created shortly after you switched to the Federal Reserve system, or the fact that the Federal Reserve is a private institution, not a government institution, and that it answers to no one! That's beyond the scope of this discussion. But there's a lot more going on behind the scenes than most people ever realize. You don't have a democracy here. The people are puppets, and they act like puppets. You, however, can have a free mind, even if you don't have a free country.

GARY: All right, while we're talking about forgiveness lessons, how do you forgive yourself? I mean, you gave me a thought process about it a while back, but people keep asking me that question.

ARTEN: That's because they don't do the thought process. But that is an important question for everyone. We told you not to say you're sorry. People should catch themselves when they use certain words. If you say you're sorry, then correct yourself in your mind. You don't have to say things out loud. What you think is even more powerful than what you say, because the thought always comes first, even if you don't articulate it. So think this in your mind, because this is how the Holy Spirit corrects you:

> *I am innocent, and nothing has happened*
> *The Holy Spirit knows What I am*
> *I am awakening in God*

When you think this way, you cannot help but have your unconscious mind undergo a healing by the Holy Spirit.

PURSAH: People have to remember that events in a dream do appear to happen, but that doesn't mean that they're real. You had dreams in bed last night that seemed so real that for all intents and purposes, that dream was reality for you. It's only when you awakened that you understood it wasn't true.

Just as you have two interpretations of other people—the ego's interpretation and the Holy Spirit's interpretation—there are also two interpretations of you. Most people choose the ego's version because they don't know there's a better way. But once you know there's a better way, you've got to go *all* the way. J didn't stop with exposing the ego or describing the problem. Anyone can describe the problem, but they don't give you a way out. They don't give you any resolution. They don't show you the way home. So then they're stuck with analyzing the problem, and when they do that, they make it real.

GARY: Yeah, and that's what the world does with everything. We study and analyze it, and we think that the most learned people are the ones whose research analyzes it the most. Scientists and physicists analyze, as well as doctors, engineers, psychoanalysts, and on and on. And all they do is testify to the reality of the illusion. So the kind of forgiveness they think of, if they think of forgiveness at all, is the kind that makes it real. "Yet no one can forgive a sin that he believes is real,"[9] according to the J guy in the Text. That's why we don't want to analyze what we're forgiving. We don't want to dwell on it. We just *notice* it, overlook it, and replace it with the truth.

So J didn't stop with the paralysis of analysis. He went all the way with this. He *completely* replaced the thought system of the ego with the thought system of the Holy Spirit, and taught that spiritual sight is thinking outside of the box, outside of the system completely. By looking *beyond* the veil to a reality that is outside of the dream that you can awaken to, it's possible to change your identity from being a body to being something that is totally unlimited, changeless, and eternal.

PURSAH: Very good, because if you teach the kind of forgiveness that makes it real, then you're not really teaching *A Course in Miracles*. How many *Course* teachers do you see out there—including the most famous ones who are on TV—talk about forgiveness, yet they never get into what real forgiveness is? That's why they're on TV, because they *don't* go all the way with this. They still make it real. They're safe. You're not on TV because you do go all the way with it. You don't make it real. You're not safe.

You tell the truth, and so you're too radical for the pop spirituality crowd. Embrace that. Somebody's got to do it.

As for the others, when they have the guided guts to go out there on TV and tell people what the *Course* actually says—that there is no world; that we forgive people not because they've really done something, but because they haven't really done anything because they don't exist; and that the unconscious mind will never be healed until you know the difference between reality and the dream, and are loyal to only one of those things in your mind—then they can call themselves *A Course in Miracles* teachers.

And *you*, dear brother, must think beyond the veil, and teach others to do so. It's not enough to describe the error. You've got to have something to replace it with. People must be communicated to that they will never find spiritual sight with the body's eyes, but by the way they think. As the *Course* teaches: "The body's eyes see only form. They cannot see beyond what they were made to see. And they were made to look on error and not see past it."[10]

The mind must be trained to choose consistently that which cannot be seen, but which can be recognized as the truth and experienced.

GARY: So in a way you could say that the purpose of the half a million words in the *Course* is to get us to an experience that is *beyond* all words.

There was no world that was here before you came here.

ARTEN: Excellent. And don't forget, if there is no world, then there was no world that was here before you came here, and there is no world that will be here for you to leave behind when you go. It never existed, and neither did you as a separate being. What you really are, and what you always will be, is perfect spirit, in a condition of perfect oneness with your Creator. Always remember this:

The ego denies the truth
The Holy Spirit denies the ego
The choice for Holiness is mine

So the *Course* is a discipline where you quit the ego. You catch yourself thinking with the ego and quit. Then you can join with the Holy Spirit. It's like quitting smoking. You have to quit the cigarettes before you can breathe the fresh air.

GARY: I know about that. I used to smoke a pack and a half a day. That's 30 cigarettes in a day. It takes time to smoke 30 cigarettes a day! It's been 30 years since I quit. I had to make a decision. When the mind makes a decision, it can do anything. I quit cold turkey. That's hard; it takes determination. And I see what you're saying about quitting the ego. That's even

There is no world that will be here for you to leave behind.

harder, because the ego keeps coming back. It's relentless, but not as relentless as the Holy Spirit. In fact, you could say that the *Course* is relentlessly uncompromising, and that no matter how hard the ego tries, the Holy Spirit's answer will always prevail.

PURSAH: Yes, and the Holy Spirit knows everything. Those conferences that you speak at—what are the longest lines of people that you see?

GARY: The longest lines I see are people waiting to talk to a psychic, or to have their tarot cards read. People want to be told what to do, and most of them have the same kinds of questions. "How can I find my soul mate?" "How can I find the right career?"

PURSAH: Yes, and even if they get an answer from a psychic or a card reader that works for them, they'd still have another question soon, and they'd have to go back to the psychic or card reader again and again. And if they're lucky, they might get a good answer half the time. But what if they had a source they could go to that was always available and always right, not just half the time or less? If they were more in spirit and had access to the inspiration of the Holy Spirit, they'd have a constant supply of answers that would always lead them to what's best for them and also for everyone else.

GARY: I'm very clear that I've been guided by the Holy Spirit and that I'm exactly where I'm supposed to be, even if I'm not in Hawaii like I expected.

ARTEN: You have work to do here, but that doesn't rule out the possibility of you living in Hawaii someday, even if it's just part of the year.

GARY: I know people who live part of the year in Hawaii and part of the year here on the West Coast—or as some people who are into politics call us, the *left coast*. But that's cool that I could live in Hawaii sometime. I love to walk there. It's great to walk here, too, but the water's warm there, and the breeze at night caresses your face, even in the winter, instead of slapping you in the face like in the Northeast. And even though it's usually warm here, most people don't know that the ocean in California is cold because the water comes down from the north, which is the opposite of how it works on the East Coast. But I'm not complaining. People come here for their vacation, and I get to live here. L.A., Hollywood, Beverly Hills, Malibu, Santa Monica, Venice Beach . . . they're all right here. We're in a great location: we can get to the airport in 20 minutes and walk to excellent restaurants. It's fantastic. Too bad our neighborhood—Brentwood—was made infamous by O.J.

NOTE: Cindy and I live just down the street from the scene of the crime that O.J. Simpson was accused of committing. The grisly murders of Nicole Brown Simpson and Ronald Goldman weren't typical of the community of Brentwood, which is quiet, has a low crime rate, and is a place where people walk late at night without fear.

ARTEN: Remember, it's your experience that matters, not the images that people have of places or of you. You're undoing the ego. That's an accomplishment. You're making a genuine contribution to humanity by assisting in the healing of not only your own mind, but of the entire mind. Not a lot of people in history have done the kind of forgiveness where you're coming from a place of cause and not effect. It's a new development in history that there are a sizable amount of people who are actually doing that. They may not put you in the history books, but so what? Most of the people in the history books were war makers—you and your readers are peacemakers. That's something.

GARY: Or if you're into the *Course,* you could say that's nothing—isn't that something? Ha, ha.

PURSAH: Yes, you're a laugh a minute. What was it that Cindy said when you went to jury duty? There's never a dull moment with Gary!

NOTE: I had been called to jury duty at the same L.A. court-house where O.J. had been tried, and I brought a Bible with me. When the prosecutors and lawyers for the defense made the selections, they could each excuse a certain amount of jurors who they didn't think would be good for their side. When asked by the prosecutor if I would be able vote guilty if the evidence warranted it, I said *no* in all sincerity and pointed out that Jesus said in the Bible: "Judge not, that ye be not judged." The prosecutor objected to me serving, and I was excused from jury duty. The judge didn't look pleased, but fortunately for me, he didn't hold me in contempt.

GARY: What was the quote? "To thine own self be true." But most people don't know the rest of it: "And it must follow, as the night the day, / Thou canst not then be false to any man." Did you know those words were written by William Tecumseh Shakespeare?

ARTEN: So you know what it means then?

GARY: Sure, it's really about consistency. In fact the *Course* itself says—wait, it's in the Manual—that honesty "actually means consistency. There is nothing you say that contradicts what you think or do; no thought opposes any other thought; no act belies your word; and no word lacks agreement with another. Such are the truly honest. At no level are they in conflict with themselves. Therefore it is impossible for them to be in conflict with anyone or anything."[11]

I joke with J a lot. I'll say, "Gee, why don't you set the bar a little higher?" His consistency was perfect. I think I still have a little more practice to do. But that's okay. I don't have anything better to do.

PURSAH: No, you don't. Undoing the ego and sharing the truth of the *Course* with others is the most you could hope for.

That's why we keep coming to see you, or for you to see us. The purpose of this series of visits, like the second series, is to continue and accelerate the undoing of the ego in you and in others. That's also the purpose of your workshops. Yes, when we speak with you there is some repetition, which is necessary to learn the *Course* and have it sink in. Even then, it won't sink in if you don't do your forgiveness work, but repetition is vital.

It's been said that the Text of *A Course in Miracles* is six pages repeated a hundred different ways.

GARY: Technically, to be statistically accurate, that would be six pages repeated 111 different ways.

PURSAH: Arten, should we say something or just stare at him?

ARTEN: Let's just stare at him.

NOTE: 30 seconds later . . .

PURSAH: Repetition appears to exist in time, but if the right message is being repeated, it undoes time. Time, like space, is just a separation idea. You have different times and different places. Yet there's no such thing. *Everything* in the universe of time and space is based on separation. Everything has a beginning and an end, a border or a limit. You've got to learn to not be taken in by the seeming impressiveness of the universe. We're not saying you can't enjoy it; you just can't make it real.

GARY: I can see that. When I go to the movies I know it's not real, but that doesn't stop me from enjoying it. That's what this movie can be like, too. Just because you know it's not true, it doesn't have to stop you from having a good time. I've been a musician my whole life, and I enjoy listening to music today more than ever. We just went to see the Eagles at the Hollywood Bowl, and we had a blast.

PURSAH: Actually, if you undo the ego, you'll end up enjoying your life more, not less. That's because there's less unconscious guilt in your mind, and if you feel less guilty you enjoy everything more, and I do mean everything. So always remember, it's not against the rules to have a good time. J, Mary, Thaddaeus, Isaah and I, Stephen, Phillip, and even Peter—we used to go into town and laugh so hard people thought we must have been drunk. But we weren't. Sometimes some of us would get feeling a little good. We drank wine. But it's not like there was clean drinking water. It wasn't unusual for people to die from drinking bad water or eating food that was too old.

GARY: Sounds like a pretty dismal existence.

ARTEN: If your happiness was dependent on circumstances, then it usually was a dismal existence back then, unless you were royalty. And people today live better than royalty did back then, but they don't appreciate it, which shows you that the toys of the world don't make people truly happy. It may excite them temporarily, but it always fades. Still, if you undo the guilt in your mind, you can be joyous. You'll also suffer less. Remember, and this cannot be emphasized enough, the *Course* says, "The guiltless mind cannot suffer."[12]

GARY: Yeah, but what about me?

ARTEN: That means that if you have absolutely no unconscious guilt in your mind, which would be the case if your mind has been completely healed by the Holy Spirit, which it would be if you have finished all of your forgiveness lessons successfully, then you would literally not be able to feel any physical pain. At the time of the Crucifixion, J couldn't feel any pain whatsoever. He could not suffer. That's just one reason why the idea of him suffering and sacrificing himself for the sins of others is the biggest myth in human history. He couldn't suffer, and sacrifice wasn't a part of his perception. A body can sacrifice itself, if you identify with it, but the lesson of the Crucifixion was that J could not be hurt, because he was not a body. He didn't identify himself with the body. In his mind he was experiencing his perfect oneness with God. What he really was could not *be* killed. It's possible for you to experience that. Imagine appearing to walk the earth as J did, and as Pursah and I did in our final lifetime, feeling completely invulnerable and totally fearless?

At the same time, Pursah and I lived a normal life. We knew how to have a good time, like you, and like Thomas, Isaah, and Thaddaeus 2,000 years ago. We weren't always the pious people the way it was represented in the New Testament. There was no such thing as a New Testament then; that came later. The time of J was still old times, like the old scripture. As Thaddaeus alluded to, those people knew how to go forth and multiply!

GARY: That's the way of the Lord

PURSAH: You still have a good time, but your life has changed Are you forgiving your latest example of culture shock?

GARY: Well, there have been a lot of changes, mostly for the good, except I haven't cut back enough on my traveling to focus on writing. Sorry about that.

PURSAH: Remember what we said about the word *sorry*.

GARY: Oh, sorry. Anyway, I love my new family. Thanksgiving is a good example of the new experience. When I was in Maine, I'd go to my in-laws' house with Karen, and her mom and dad would be there, of course, until her dad passed away, and her brothers and their families were there; and practically all we talked about was sports. I can talk about sports for an hour, but I don't want to talk about it for six hours. Now it's totally different. Cindy and I spend the holiday with her sister, Jackie, and their mom at Jackie's place. Jackie is a hypnotherapist and *Course* student, and Cindy's mom, Doris, is a longtime student of the *Course;* they've read our books, like Cindy, and most of the time we talk about the *Course!* It's really different from my life in Maine, which feels like a past life now, but I guess we all live several lifetimes within this one dream lifetime.

NOTE: Since then, the four of us have been joined by Mark, who met Jackie on a cruise to Mexico that I was sponsoring for my readers. They were married about eight months later. Mark is also a dedicated student of the *Course,* and a retired Air Force Major who flew huge cargo planes and trained pilots in Afghanistan. He's also an accomplished musician, as well as a recording and video producer. Mark has a recording studio in his home. I consider him to be a brother as well as a brother-in-law, and I can't help but notice that he uses both sides of his illusory brain.

GARY: When I was a kid in Massachusetts, the whole family would get together—maybe 40 people at my uncle's house, and most of us could play an instrument or sing, or both, and there would be a big jam session. That seems like so long ago now. I can't believe I'm going to be 60. I feel like I'm in my 30s.

ARTEN: Did you notice that you haven't aged since we started appearing to you? It will soon be 20 years since we first showed up.

GARY: I never thought of it that way. I just figured I looked young, but you're right. Is that because you broke my thought patterns, and I started practicing true forgiveness?

ARTEN: Yes, you think you've been through a lot, but the stress has been nothing for you compared to what it would have been. It's not the situation. Everyone experiences what leads to stressful situations. It's always how you look at it that matters.

GARY: I wanted to ask you something. I've been thinking of trying to get a movie made out of the books, but there's so much information that it may be too much to put into a film. Do you think a TV series would be better?

PURSAH: We're not going to tell you that. We want you to go through the process. It's part of your script, no pun intended, and we want you to experience what you're supposed to go through. Ask the Holy Spirit what you should do. You'll be guided to what's best for everyone.

GARY: How's this for an idea? I can see you and Arten, guns blazing, being chased by the bad guys through Salt Lake City. Then you crash in Temple Square and there's a three-way shoot-out between you, the bad guys, and renegade members of the Mormon Tabernacle Choir.

PURSAH: It needs work. You were talking about culture shock.

GARY: Oh yeah. After awhile you get used to seeing famous people, and having five lanes on each side of the freeway, and you start to find the little out-of-the-way gems that are the real California. It hasn't been bad. In fact, most of the time it's been good, except it's really expensive here. I think the travel part has been the hardest ever since this whole thing started. I mean, when I started traveling, I was treated like a customer, but now I'm treated like a suspect. Every year they find another way to make things more difficult for travelers. That's been a big forgiveness op for me. When I saw Cindy being patted down, I really started to get pissed off.

ARTEN: And Cindy?

GARY: I'll tell you, Cindy was so angry, she almost said something.

ARTEN: But not really.

GARY: Nah. She's the most positive person I've ever met. You know that Workbook lesson number 68—love holds no grievances? That's her.

ARTEN: Yes, you're very lucky. And when something comes up to forgive, as it always does in a marriage, don't forget what it's for. If you use it as the Holy Spirit would have you use it, and think of the other person as being what they really are, then you'll have a Holy relationship.

GARY: Yeah, and we can enjoy the movie, too, including travel. For example, I had a funny experience in Denver. I was going through security, and there was this older TSA agent putting the stuff through the metal detector. He looked like he was probably in his 70s, and it made me think he had to work beyond his retirement years to make ends meet. Anyway, I just happened to be close to him and I said, "How's it going?" and he said, "I'm living the dream."

PURSAH: He was joking, and it's good that he has a sense of humor about his situation. Yet it is possible to live the happy dream that J talks about. His *Course* is a happy form of spirituality. It's not the suffering, morose, religious dogma that people are used to. In fact, it guarantees you a happy ending to this whole predicament you seem to find yourself in. You know that there's an end to time, because the *Course* teaches that the Holy Spirit looked back "from a point where time was ended."[13] When we said the Holy Spirit can see everything, we weren't kidding.

> **No one will be left out of Heaven, or else it wouldn't be whole.**

Everyone is going to the same place. No one will be left out of Heaven, or else it wouldn't be whole.

GARY: But what about these pricks who don't deserve it?

ARTEN: These brothers aren't going to Heaven as pricks, because they're not going to Heaven as bodies. They will eventually forget all about bodily identification. It was just a dream, and where is a dream when you wake up from it? It disappears. That's why we told you to call the first book *The Disappearance of the Universe.*

GARY: Oh. I always wondered why it was called that.

ARTEN: They will return to their home, which is perfect oneness. Remember something, Gary, there's no one here on Earth who wasn't a murderer at one time or another. That's duality. Do you think you should all remain in dreams of hell,[14] as the *Course* puts it?

GARY: I'm thinking. Okay, I forgot about seeming opposites. A lot of people are concerned about the idea of going to hell. They don't realize they're already there. According to J, anything that isn't the perfect oneness of Heaven is hell. And you know, when you think about it, all the scary things you see in those old books that have drawings of hell—people burning and being decapitated and stuff—can actually happen to you here! You don't have to go to hell for that, because if you're not in Heaven then you are in hell. But since what is all encompassing can have no opposite,[15] hell doesn't really exist, not anywhere, despite any appearances.

PURSAH: A flash of brilliance. So tell me, what was your impression the very first time you picked up the *Course* in that New Age bookstore in Auburn, Maine, and read a little bit of it?

GARY: I thought, *What the hell is this?* I mean, it may as well have been written in a foreign language. That reminds me, when we—Cindy and I—went to Athens, Greece, and I was doing a workshop, I asked the people, "When we don't understand something like the *Course,* we say, 'It's all Greek to me.' What do *you* say?" They said, "Chinese."

PURSAH: And why do you think the *Course* is so hard to understand?

GARY: You mean aside from the half-million words that are in scholarly, Freudian, biblical language, and the iambic pentameter—and the teachings that are so wild and heavy that they give people physical symptoms?

PURSAH: Yes, aside from that.

GARY: I don't know.

ARTEN: It's so hard to understand because it's a holographic presentation. It doesn't spell things out for you in a linear manner. The *Course* starts out with its most advanced principles. Look at number one in the Principles of Miracles section. It says, "There is no order of difficulty in miracles."[16] There's no way that anyone could read that and have any idea what it means.

First of all, you don't even know what a miracle is yet. The reason J called it *A Course in Miracles* was because he wanted to change the definition of the word *miracle*. Instead of people thinking a miracle is something that happens out there on the screen you call the world—which is just the effect, like the burning bush, for example—he wanted people to start thinking of a miracle as something that happens in the mind, which is cause. Yes, the miracle may or may not show up as a symbol on the screen, but the real miracle takes place when you change your mind and practice true forgiveness with the Holy Spirit instead of thinking with the ego.

Now, through repetition, you hopefully start to catch on to what the *Course* is really saying, but as you know, that's rare. So what we do with your books is we give you and others a linear presentation of the *Course*. We spell it out for you. We get you to understand it to the point where you can go back and read it for yourself and it makes sense to you.

GARY: I believe that. I've talked to countless people who gave up on the *Course* and had it sitting on their bookshelves at home for years, and then they read our books and went back to the *Course* because they got it. You can't apply something to your life if you don't understand it, but now they did. That alone makes all the crap I've had to go through worth it.

ARTEN: What you or anyone else goes through is worth it only if you forgive it. Always remember what it's for. So the purpose of our work is to give a linear presentation of the *Course* that empowers people to grasp it in such a way that they can read it, understand it, and do it.

GARY: Got it. And that thing about the Holy Spirit looking back from the end of time—that's pretty out there, in a very cool way.

ARTEN: The *Course's* view of time is mind bending. That's because time has a paradox. On the one hand, time is holographic. Everything happens all at once and, according to the *Course,* it's already over. Past, present, and future occur simultaneously, as Einstein pointed out, and which the *Course* would agree with, except the *Course* would say it just appeared to occur. Then, aside from the holographic model, there's the false experience of linearity. By the way, the holographic model is false, too, because ultimately, as we said, time is just a separation idea.

So your experience is that events happen one after another. You actually believe that you're making this up as you go along. I'm not saying that's not people's experience. It is. I'm just saying that it's a *false* experience. What you're seeing is not true. Where does that leave you? It means that even though it's already happened, you've still got to do it!

GARY: Yeah, one of my favorite lines in the *Course* is in Workbook lesson number 169. J gives us all this esoteric stuff about time, and how the Holy Spirit "wrote salvation's script in His Creator's Name, and in the Name of His Creator's Son."[17] That would be Christ, who is me when I'm not here, and this was the Answer to the ego's script, and all that. Then comes my favorite line. J says, "There is no need to further clarify what no one in the world can understand."[18] I love that. I mean, what the hell did he bring it up for in the first place?

ARTEN: Incidentally, the script that the Holy Spirit wrote does not take place in the world. Remember, there is no world! And I think you know that even though this is a course in cause and not effect, the first thing most *Course* teachers and students do is take the *Course* and put it right out there on the screen and make it about fixing the world. So now they're going to save a world that isn't there. No. The Holy Spirit's script is a different *interpretation* of the ego's script. The ego's script is what happens. You could also call it karma. That's a false, illusory cause and effect that seems to happen on the screen, including what appears to happen to your own body. But even the body is just an effect. It's a symptom, a symbol of separation.

The Holy Spirit's script takes place in the mind. You learn how to use your one real power and choose the Holy Spirit's interpretation of what you're seeing. When you do that, you're switching to the Holy Spirit's script, which comes to you from outside of time and space, and changes your mind about time and space.

GARY: Wow. I think I actually get that. Does that mean I'm spiritually advanced?

PURSAH: Don't make us stare at you again.

GARY: Sometimes people ask me what the best way to do the *Course* is: they want to know, for instance, should they do the Text first or the Workbook first; do they have to do the Workbook in one year, or can they take longer; if they don't think they're doing it right, should they start over, and things like that.

ARTEN: First, if they've read *Disappearance*, or D.U., as many of your readers call it, then they can start with the Workbook. They'll understand it pretty well if they've read your first book, and even better if they've read your second book, and soon the one we're doing now. Also, they don't have to do the Workbook in just one year. You took a year plus four and a half months the first time you did it. Sometimes you find a Workbook lesson that's particularly helpful to you, so you stick with it for a few days, or you take a couple of days off. It's all right. As you know, the only rule is you can't do more than one lesson in a day.

In addition, when you do the Workbook, don't stop and start over again like so many people do. They think they're not doing it right. But no one is going to do the Workbook as well as they think they should. If they did the Workbook perfectly, I'd question what the hell they're doing here in the first place. Just do it the best you can. Convincing you that you're not doing the Workbook right, and then getting you to start over again, is one of the ego's ways of trying to trick you into not doing it.

As for the Text, remember how you tried to read it very fast at first?

GARY: Yeah, that was stupid. I didn't understand much. Although I could see it was J speaking in the first person because I had read the Bible some.

ARTEN: The best way to read the Text is slowly. Read about two pages a day. Don't rush it. If you read two pages or less a day, you'll still read the whole Text in less than a year. You can even take days off every now and then. You'll understand it better, and you can make it practical, like the Workbook. Instead of it being just theory, you can take the ideas you read and apply them to your everyday life, when it's appropriate. That's what the *Course* calls right-minded thinking. You're thinking with the Holy Spirit. You're breaking the ego's thought patterns. This eventually changes your experience of life, because you're dealing with the cause.

Do the same with the Manual for Teachers. Take your time, and read two pages a day. Let it sink in. Get used to thinking like the Holy Spirit, and you will return to spirit.

The Holy Instant is that second when you choose the Holy Spirit instead of the ego.

PURSAH: We've said the *Course* teaches that Heaven is changeless and eternal. We've also said that the Holy Instant is that second when you choose the Holy Spirit instead of the ego. Remember, then, these words from the chapter of the Text called The Holy Instant:

> Time is inconceivable without change, yet holiness does not change. Learn from this instant more than merely that hell does not exist. In this redeeming instant lies Heaven. And Heaven will not change, for the birth into the holy present is salvation from change.[19]

GARY: Thanks. It's good to know Heaven won't ever change—that there's something you can depend on forever. It's also good to know for sure that true forgiveness is the way to get there. You know, I've met people who have been studying the *Course* for five years, and they still don't know it's about forgiveness—true forgiveness, that is. They get fascinated by the metaphysics, or distracted by teachers who don't really get it, and the result is they can't see the forest through the trees.

ARTEN: Don't forget, there's tremendous unconscious resistance to really getting this and doing it. It's not a matter of intelligence; it's a question of the ego's resistance. This is death to the ego, and on some level the ego senses it. And the ego will come up with a thousand different ways to distract you from the truth. Of course its first goal is to convince you that you're a body, but it will come up with many other distractions as well. As far as the ego is concerned, anything that delays you from experiencing the truth will do.

GARY: You mean like that whole controversy about earlier versions of the *Course* supposedly being the right versions instead of the Foundation for Inner Peace edition that most people are familiar with?

PURSAH: Yes. That's exactly what the *Course* is talking about when it describes controversy as, "a defense against truth in the form of a delaying maneuver."[20] Most of the differences among the versions are in the first five chapters, which had personal and professional material in them that was meant for the scribes, which they wanted removed. But the Text of the *Course* doesn't have 5 chapters—it has 31 chapters, and that's not mentioning the Workbook and the Manual for Teachers. Talk about not seeing the forest through the trees!

The *Course* was a work in progress for seven years. Bill Thetford, Helen's trusted friend and colleague, typed it out once as Helen relayed J's dictation from her shorthand notebook to him. But Helen typed it out six more times in the six years after that, always being edited by J. By 1972, when Helen first showed parts of the *Course* to Ken Wapnick, she had already completed any editing of content. The only editing Helen did with Ken was for consistent capitalization, punctuation, chapter titles, and subtitles. Ken never did any editing of content, and Bill was never interested in being an editor. His only contribution was to change the first 51 principles of miracles to 50 by combining two of them, because he thought it looked better. Aside from that, he did no editing.

Some people want to make a big deal out of the fact that one of the earlier versions, the "urtext," says that if there's any disagreement about what should go in the *Course,* Bill should be the one to decide. There's one thing these people don't tell you though, because they weren't there, and that is there never was any disagreement between Helen and Bill as to what should go in the *Course.* They knew what it meant, so it was self-evident to them what should be in the *Course.* And don't forget that Helen and Bill came to California in the late '70s to introduce the *Course* here. They appeared with, used, and supported the edition published by the Foundation for Inner Peace, of which they were founding members, along with Ken Wapnick, Bob Skutch, and Judy Skutch, now, of course, Judy Skutch Whitson.

The earlier versions of the *Course* that have become available include material that was stolen from the U.S. Copyright Office and the library of the Association for Research and Enlightenment in Virginia Beach. There's no integrity in that. How would you like it if you went through the whole process of writing a book, had it published, and then someone stole your first draft, put it out illegally on the Internet, and then claimed that this was the right version of the book, and that you were selling the wrong version?! Yet that's exactly what happened with the *Course.* And because a rather confused judge—who described the *Course* as "sophomoric"—later invalidated its copyright and put it in the public domain, today people are free to sell the earlier drafts and make money off of stolen material. If you want to support that, then be my guest. Or you can stick with the real thing, which was given to Helen over a period of seven years as J constantly corrected her, just as the Holy Spirit is constantly correcting you.

GARY: Tell me how you really feel. Hey, not to change the subject, but if Mary was enlightened like J, did she do any of the kinds of seemingly miraculous things he did, like raising the dead and stuff?

PURSAH: Yes, she was enlightened, and she did do miraculous things. Of course the miracle takes place in the mind, which is cause, and it shows up in the world, which is effect. Now you don't have to raise the dead like J did in order to be enlightened. If everyone went around raising the dead, then nobody would ever die, and you'd all be stuck here forever. Mary did bring her cat back to life when it died—not that any person or animal ever really dies, but Mary felt guided to bring her cat back, and she did. It lived for a couple of days, and Mary was very happy.

At one point J and Mary walked on water together.

GARY: Together!

PURSAH: Yes, it really shocked the people who saw it, including Thaddaeus and me. It was very unexpected, to say the least. It happened just a couple of days before they were married. J was 27, and Mary was 22. That was actually rather old for people to get married at the time, but it was meant to be.

GARY: The script is written.

PURSAH: Yes. They didn't do that to induce belief. They did it to demonstrate that the laws of this world do not apply when you know how to use the power of the mind with the Holy Spirit's guidance. As J would put it later in his *Course,* "Through your holiness the power of God is made manifest. Through your holiness the power of God is made available. And there is nothing the power of God cannot do."[21]

Isaah and I did get to go to J and Mary's wedding. That's when I gave him a scroll and a writing instrument as a present. J and I knew how to read and write, but most people didn't. He gave both things right back to me and said, "Travel with me. Use these things to be my scribe." I was so happy when I heard that. It felt right, and Isaah, who loved the five of us being together—that includes Thaddaeus—was all for the idea. The next few years were the most exciting of our lives, because we got to make a contribution in sharing the message of the Holy Spirit with others, and learn it ourselves from J and Mary at the same time.

J and Mary could also use mind transport to go anywhere in the world instantly. J really did go to a lot of the places people think he did, such as India, Tibet, China, and even France and England. He and Mary liked Stonehenge. They knew energy wasn't real, but they could still appreciate it, as well as the astronomical-astrological plan behind the whole thing.

GARY: I know. I've been there!

PURSAH: Yes, but you didn't see it in its original form. The first thousand years or so it was whole, and the stones weren't just the ones that were standing; they were also covered with stones and they made up a complete circle. J and Mary went there one morning and joined with God. Then they levitated and disappeared, which left quite an impression on the few people who saw them.

GARY: When I was in Greece, someone told me J visited there during his lifetime.

ARTEN: Yes, Greece wasn't that far away, and even though they used mind transport, they could have gone there without it. People traveled longer distances in those days than folks today realize. We had trade routes that went halfway around the world, but J and Mary took the easy way.

It's known by some that Saul, or St. Paul, spoke about 20 years after the Crucifixion at the Parthenon in Athens. What is not widely known is that J also spoke there, about 25 years before that. The people were amazed by his wisdom.

We're talking about a guy who was 12 years old when he spoke with the rabbis in the Temple in Jerusalem. And they addressed him as *rabbi,* which means teacher. You could not get a higher compliment from a rabbi than to have him call you rabbi. Anyway, when a master comes back for their final lifetime, there isn't a big learning curve. They already know pretty much everything they need to know in order to be enlightened. Usually, they just have one big lesson to teach and learn—in J's case, the Crucifixion—and they are also there to be a light that guides others in the right direction. You can't help but be an influence on people when you practice true forgiveness, because every mind is joined. You can't do other people's forgiveness work for them, but you can act as an example.

Now let's play a game.

GARY: A game? You're not gonna zap me around the universe again, are you? I have a chiropractor appointment.

ARTEN: No. Tell us things that you've learned from the *Course,* or that you've experienced as a result of doing the *Course.* Just put it out there, like free association, except do it like you're giving us a list. Obviously it won't be anything close to what you've actually learned, but it will be a sample. We'll tell you why later.

GARY: Okay, let me think.

PURSAH: Don't think.

GARY: Well, sometimes when you ask people who have done something really amazing, "Hey, how did you get the idea to do that?" they'll say, "Oh, it just came to me." That's an inspired idea. It just comes to you. It doesn't feel like you're the one who thought of it. The idea just comes into your mind. And then you act on it, and it works. That's when you start to get excited about those kinds of ideas, because you realize you have guidance that will always be there for you, and it will work.

People think the *Course* takes a long time. That's because they want instant gratification. But if they get that gratification, they're not gratified, because it doesn't make them happy, except maybe for a few days. In truth, 10 or 20 years are nothing in the overall scheme of things. It took us a few million years, just in the human-being part of history, which is a drop in the bucket, to get used to thinking with the ego. To undo all of that in just one or two lifetimes *is* an absolute miracle.

I was doing a workshop, and there was a lady in the audience who was 80 years old. I told the crowd it could take ten years to get really good at practicing forgiveness. It's like playing a musical instrument. It takes time, and you have to practice every day. She came up to me during the break and said, "Ten years? If it takes me ten years to do this, I'll be 90!" I thought for a few seconds, and then asked her, "How old will you be in ten years if you *don't* do it?"

Later I was talking about undoing the ego, and awakening, and I asked the audience members, "So what if it takes time? You haven't got anything better to do."

Sometimes at a workshop, if I think of it, when we break for lunch, I tell everyone not to eat too much. People use food as a tranquilizer, and pigging out makes you drowsy. We don't have to eat as much as we think we do. It's another way the ego conspires to root us in the body. Come to think of it, I'll bet J and Mary didn't eat much.

The *Course* says, "Heaven is the decision I must make."[22] So you've got to do it yourself. Make the decision that Heaven is where you're going, and awakening as fast as you can through forgiveness is the way to get there. There's nothing outside of you that will do that for you. There's no reason to be happy, so be happy for no reason.

When I'm thinking with the Holy Spirit, it's like I'm above the battleground.[23] I love the part in the Text about that. It's like you're not stuck in it—you're unattached.

The word *Namaste* was not meant to be a separation idea, as we discussed earlier. When people think of what it means—the divinity in me bows down to the divinity in you—it's like, you've got your divinity over there and I've got my divinity over here, and don't touch my divinity. But what the word *divinity* is referring to is really perfect oneness.

History is just a story. It never happened, and neither did today or tomorrow.

It's not the goal of the *Course* to make anything happen in the world. But there's an irony; if you're undoing the ego and you have more access to spirit, it's more likely for you to be guided to good things in the world. That's not guaranteed, however. You look at J at the end of his life; things weren't exactly going good. The point was it didn't matter.

> **You can't undo your experience of scarcity without undoing the idea of separation from God.**

You can't undo your experience of scarcity without undoing the idea of separation from God. As long as you're experiencing separation, you'll never really feel abundant. When you undo the experience of separation, you'll never feel lack. You'll feel abundant even if you're broke. But with separation, you'll feel scarcity even if you're rich.

I love J. He really sticks to the *Course.*

Judy Skutch and Ken Wapnick, people who were there even before the *Course* was published, have always been very nice to me. I appreciate their kindness

We wouldn't have any fear of death if we didn't have an unconscious fear of God.

Christianity is full of violent images. I was in South Carolina and I saw a billboard with a drawing of Jesus nailed to the cross. He looked kind of buffed and angry. The caption with the words they put in his mouth was: "You drew first blood, but I'm coming back." I guess that's Rambo Jesus.

I was in Santa Barbara and heard the story of Saint Barbara. Apparently, her father chopped her head off, and later, he was struck by lightning. Today, statues of Saint Barbara in town show her holding a lightning bolt. Violent chick, for a saint.

Because of guilt, losing hurts more than winning feels good.

Two thousand years ago, J said, "If you had faith enough you could move mountains." Most people don't know what he said next: "But where are you going to put them?"

My former wife, Karen, has always supported my books and all of my work. I'm very grateful for that. She even gives copies of my books to people.

PURSAH: You can stop there. It's good to think that way sometimes. Just rattle off right-minded things you've learned and observed. It reinforces right-minded thinking. And it's all right to acknowledge how far you've come. You were in pretty bad shape when you were in your 20s. Be grateful for what's happened for you since then.

GARY: I hear you.

NOTE: It seems my life has run in 14-year cycles. And I know from trading the markets and observing the world, that everything runs in cycles. From the time I was born to the time I was 14, my life was pretty good. People liked me; I was smart, I could run fast, I was a good baseball player, and I had friends. I had scoliosis and didn't know it. I could have bursts of energy that enabled me to run like the wind for short distances, but I had no stamina. I was only really fast for a hundred yards.

Then when I was 14, I started to become depressed, and it became worse as the years went on. By the time I hit my 20s it was a miserable existence. For 14 years I didn't know what was wrong with me, or that my thoughts over the years had made my experience.

When I was 28, I did the est training. The next 14 years were a great learning experience for me. My thought patterns were broken by est, and my first thought system empowered me to change my life.

Fourteen years later, I was in Maine. At the age of 42, I was finally ready to learn *A Course in Miracles* from Arten and Pursah. That set up a different kind of 14-year learning period. Their nine-year introductory period in which I went from knowing nothing about the *Course* to learning and applying it to my life ensured that I would never be the same. When I was 52, D.U. was published, and from then on my life would *definitely* never be the same.

At the age of 56, it was time for another 14-year cycle to begin for me. I did what for me was the unthinkable for almost all of my life. I moved to California. This was a new cycle for sure. Would it turn out to be a place of joy, or would it turn out to be one great big giant forgiveness lesson? The script would reveal itself. Was I ready?

And what would happen when I was 70, the beginning of cycle number five? Would I move to Hawaii? So much of my life had revealed itself, yet so much was unknown. Because of Arten and Pursah, I sometimes felt like I knew more about my next and final lifetime than I did the future of this one.

And now I was with Cindy. The *Course* spoke strikingly about the difference between a special relationship and a holy one. We both knew the difference. Could we forge a holy relationship? I felt that if we couldn't, then nobody could. Yet J's descriptions of special relationships seemed to make the challenge a daunting one, as with this poignant passage from the *Course:*

Who has need for sin? Only the lonely and alone, who see their brothers different from themselves. It is this difference, seen but not real, that makes the need for sin, not real but seen, seem justified. And all this would be real if sin were so. For an unholy relationship is based on differences, where each one thinks the other has what he has not. They come together, each to complete himself and rob the other. They stay until they think that there is nothing left to steal, and then move on. And so they wander through a world of strangers, unlike themselves, living with their bodies perhaps under a common roof that shelters neither; in the same room and yet a world apart.[24]

I knew that passage described most of the couples in the world, yet it was possible to see beyond the veil, to never be alone because of differences, and to be fulfilled by oneness. As the *Course* said, in the same section:

A holy relationship starts from a different premise. Each one has looked within and seen no lack. Accepting his completion, he would extend it by joining with another, whole as himself. He sees no difference between these selves, for differences are only of the body. Therefore, he looks on nothing he would take. He denies not his own reality *because* it is the truth. Just under Heaven does he stand, but close enough not to return to earth. For this relationship has Heaven's holiness. How far from home can a relationship so like to Heaven be?[25]

So there was hope. With spiritual sight, which is the result of true forgiveness, it was possible to live together under one roof, in the same room, yet recognizing the wholeness of Heaven, and never apart.

GARY: I *am* grateful, believe me, even if I do forget to be grateful sometimes. Plus, living with the *Course* is fun. You can joke about the world and its foolishness without being too harsh.

PURSAH: Especially since it was never here.

GARY: Right. So if I eat that apple on the coffee table over there, and it's gone, then it doesn't matter because it was never really there in the first place.

PURSAH: That's correct.

GARY: And if I had an assault rifle, and it was banned, then it wouldn't really matter because *that* was never really there in the first place.

PURSAH: Yes, and I think you should bring that up at the next meeting of the National Rifle Association. I'm sure it would transform the entire event.

ARTEN: You'll notice that no matter what we talk about in these discussions, sooner or later we always bring the conversation back around to true forgiveness. That's what accelerates your process of awakening the most. As you know, learning and applying this kind of forgiveness, which is the opposite of the way the world thinks, can be hard, especially at first. But you get used to it. It becomes a part of you. Your mind is dominated, in a good way, more and more by the Holy Spirit. "And thus are miracles as natural as fear and agony appeared to be before the choice for holiness was made."[26]

This has been a long visit for you. Take time to integrate things. You've been on a hell of a roller-coaster ride.

PURSAH: We know that our decision to not let you record our conversations this time is making it more difficult for you to write the book. Combined with everything else, it's quite a task for you. But you also know it's good for you, and that your ability to hear us between visits has improved even more. You've become quite a channel. As for the delays, don't worry about them. Just make more time for writing as you go along, and eventually you will have come full circle. You'll be back to being a writer. Thank you for being *our* scribe. We really do appreciate you, even when we rib you mercilessly.

GARY: I love you guys.

ARTEN: We love you, too, brother. We want to close this visit with a couple of paragraphs from the *Course* about the miracle of forgiveness. Be well, and keep undoing.

A miracle contains the gift of grace, for it is given and received as one. And thus it illustrates the law of truth the world does not obey, because it fails entirely to understand its ways. A miracle inverts perception which was upside down before, and thus it ends the strange distortions that were manifest. Now is perception open to the truth. Now is forqiveness seen as justified.

Forgiveness is the home of miracles. The eyes of Christ deliver them to all they look upon in mercy and in love. Perception stands corrected in His sight, and what was meant to curse has come to bless. Each lily of forgiveness offers all the world the silent miracle of love. And each is laid before the Word of God, upon the universal alter to Creator and creation in the light of perfect purity and endless joy.[27]

7

ARTEN IN THIS LIFETIME

*There is no past or future, and the idea of birth into a body
has no meaning either once or many times. Reincarnation
cannot, then, be true in any real sense. Our only question should
be, "Is the concept helpful?" And that depends, of course,
on what it is used for. If it is used to strengthen the recognition
of the eternal nature of life, it is helpful indeed.*[1]

The idea that we move from lifetime to lifetime occupying different bodies is a concept that is accepted by most people in the
world. In America, there is no accurate public-opinion poll on the
subject that I know of, but certainly there are many who believe
that they have lived before and will do so again. The idea is treated
differently in the *Course*, because it teaches that we are never actually in a body. We do not "incarnate." The body itself is just part
of the same projection as the rest of the projection of a universe
of time and space. The body appears to surround us as part of the
ego's plan of separation, but it doesn't actually exist anymore than
the rest of the world.

Thus, our lifetimes are illusory dreams of life in the body. So
while most view previous lifetimes as physical incarnations, the
Course would think of them as serial hallucinations that need to
be dispelled rather than cherished. It's very tempting to take pride

in a previous life that was seemingly important, making it, and the body, real. People who remember those lifetimes usually remember the remarkable ones and seldom recall the lifetimes they died in prison or with their face in the gutter. The ego wants to make things attractive and keep us coming back for more.

Still, the concept of reincarnation can be helpful if it's used to further the idea that this seeming lifetime is not all there is, and that life—illusory or real—does not end. As J puts it in the *Course,* what we need to recognize is that "birth was not the beginning, and death is not the end."[2] If we are mentally reviewing that which has already gone by, then even though we appear to be trapped in a body, the whole movie is a trick. There is a continuum to it in the illusory model, but none of it is real, including the body. Reincarnation, while not a fact but an illusion, does foster the notion that this life is not as important as we think because there are so many of them. At one point Arten and Pursah told me that we appear to live thousands of them. This would be in harmony with the Manual for Teachers statement that says, "There is always some good in any thought which strengthens the idea that life and the body are not the same."[3]

As the years blended into each other, I started to see the things that happened to me, and didn't happen for me, as pure and simple karma. If someone appeared to attack me in this lifetime, it was because I had attacked the person in another. If I had not been kind to certain individuals in this lifetime, it was because they had not

True forgiveness melts karma away.

been kind to me in a past that I'm not always consciously aware of, but which the unconscious mind never forgets. What was different now was that I had the tools to rise above the illusory cause and effect that is thought of as karma. True forgiveness melts karma away. The cause and effect are both undone. If the lesson is learned and resolved through forgiveness, there is no need for that lesson to return in a future dream lifetime. Bad karma disappears.

The seeming cause and effect also applies to circumstances and shows up on the screen as duality. If people are rich this time around, they had been equally poor another time. If poor, they had been rich. If healthy, they had been sickly in a previous life. If sick, they had gotten to experience glowing health at another time.

People's thoughts were always responsible for their experience of life, but *not* always responsible for what happened to them or what they received materially. I remember a long time ago hearing Woody Allen talk about his fear of flying. He hated to travel by plane. One of the ways he got through it was that he would think of the ten worst things that could possibly happen; and then, when they didn't happen, he felt better. This also helped him lessen his fear by realizing that most of the things people worry about never occur . . . but wait a minute here. If the New Age dogma says that your thoughts attract what happens to you and which material things you attract into your life, then by focusing on the negative, our friend Woody should have been killed by his negative thoughts, or at least be ruined by them, a long, long time ago. Instead, he has had an extremely successful life, full of the kind of accomplishments most people can only dream of.

There are universal happenings that demonstrate the script is written, and that people in the East are right when they conclude that whatever happens to you is your karma. There are people who are victims whom the world sees as not deserving their fate; there are those who are extremely well-off whom others think haven't earned it. Life isn't fair. Of course it's not. But there is a reason why things are the way that they are. The *Course* would probably say it's not a very good reason—that karmic justice is more a description of the problem than a solution. Our true freedom lies in looking past the illusory world and awakening to the real one. I felt like I had turned the corner, and that nothing could stop me from achieving that goal.

Ever since the day in Las Vegas when I first talked to Cindy, we stayed in touch. She had told me that I could contact her through her website. I was cool. I waited three days. I still have the first couple of e-mails we shared. There was a "bigness" about them, as though we'd always known each other and that our destinies were being played out in a way determined long ago. But I didn't tell her who I thought she was.

As time went on, I was astounded by how much we had in common. I liked Cindy's CD of original songs she had recorded in California. Not only could she write songs, but her singing and piano playing were also beautiful. When we talked about *A Course in Miracles*, her understanding of it was quite advanced. As mentioned earlier, she'd read D.U., and her relationship with her mom and sister and their discussions of the *Course* had helped her tremendously.

On the level of form, Cindy came from a very strong gene pool. Not only was her mom a doctor of both music and psychology, two areas that Cindy was also adept in, but her dad was also an award-winning history professor in Toledo, Ohio, where Cindy had grown up. I could tell from the many stories she shared that she had a happy childhood, and that she actually enjoyed going to school some of the time and had many friends, which was something I couldn't say.

I graduated from Beverly High in Beverly, Massachusetts, just a few miles from the Atlantic Ocean. Cindy also graduated from Beverly High, as the locals call it, or Beverly Hills High, as it's more commonly known, just a few miles from the Pacific Ocean. Cindy's family wasn't rich, but her mom had found a nice apartment in an area of Beverly Hills that wasn't full of mansions, but was a good middle-class section for the Ohio transplants to be in. They wouldn't be appearing on *Lifestyles of the Rich and Famous*, but that didn't seem to be very important to them.

I met Cindy in May 2006, and my second book, *Your Immortal Reality: How to Break the Cycle of Birth and Death*, was released in August of that year. One of the chapters was called "Who's Arten?" Cindy knew the part of the story of Arten and Pursah that was told in the first book. From our talks and what she read in the second book, she started to put the pieces of the puzzle together. Cindy didn't have past-life recall, and most people—including those who are spiritually advanced—do not. I didn't want to tell her she was Arten. It sounded like yet another bad pickup line: "Hey baby, you're Arten." But she was smart. She's smarter than me, but I forgave her. By the fall of that year we saw each other, and at dinner we practically said it at the same time. There was no reason to deny it. Cindy was Arten, and she was also Thaddaeus 2,000 years ago, and would live her final lifetime with me as I lived my final lifetime as Pursah, 100 years from now in Chicago. Except in that phase of the dream, we wouldn't find each other until a little later in life. A&P told me they were married to other people first, and that their spouses had passed away. Then they found each other and lived together for the rest of their lives. I wondered if they would ever share more details about those relationships and that lifetime with me. I decided I would ask them sometime.

On June 18, 2007, I landed in Southern California for the first time as a resident, and Cindy picked me up at LAX. It was an exciting, new world for me. My first night there our friends, Jerry and Rochelle, whom I had met a few months before in Hawaii, drove us to their friends' house in Laurel Canyon where we listened to a guru from India, and a famous actress gave me the "Oneness Blessing." It was surreal for me to suddenly be in the heart of the film industry, and to have a celebrity rubbing my head. I wasn't in Maine anymore.

As for the Oneness Blessing, it was a perfect example of how people decide what is going to be helpful to them, or even heal them, at the level of the mind. The Oneness Blessing does nothing, but the mind of the recipient can do anything. For example, a couple of years after the blessing, I saw a healer who was visiting the Agape International Spiritual Center in Culver City. He came out and just stared at the audience for ten minutes. His "staring" healed no one, and neither did his presence, but it was indeed possible for someone in the crowd to be healed if that person had decided on the level of the mind to get well.

In the fall of my first year in SoCal, Jerry and Rochelle organized a workshop for me at UCLA. It was there during lunch that Cindy and I met producer and writer Elysia Skye, who would work with me to try to get my books made into a film or television series. If I didn't meet Jerry and Rochelle earlier that year, I may never have met Elysia. I didn't know what the result of that collaboration would be. My teachers seldom told me about my personal future. They didn't want to rob me of my experiences or my forgiveness opportunities. But meeting and becoming friends with Elysia would have been enough of a reward on its own.

On the same trip to Hawaii where I met Jerry and Rochelle, I also met a guy named Dain; and it turned out that he lived next door to two friends of ours in Mount Shasta—Michael and Rapha-elle Tamura. It's not just a case of it being a small world. It's all connected.

Michael is a gifted medium, spiritual teacher, healer, and au-thor. He's also a "split" of mine. Arten and Pursah had explained that sometimes more than one person will have legitimate memo-ries of being a specific individual in a past life, because before the mind of that past person divided due to the idea of separation, the people with those memories were that person.

It's rare for two splits to ever meet each other, because by defi-nition they have split and gone in different directions. But Mi-chael and I did meet and became good friends. Michael, who is Japanese, has a great sense of humor and is almost always smil-ing. From the time we first met, I admired his personality and the way he was able to laugh at life. There are some "intellectual" teachers of spirituality, including teachers of the *Course,* who have forgotten to laugh. They have no sense of humor whatsoever, but Michael remembers to laugh. As Goethe wrote: "The man of un-derstanding finds all things laughable, the man of reason few."

One of the fantastic gifts of being an international speaker showed up in the form of the amazing places Cindy and I got to see in the next few years, as well as the people we met. *A Course in Miracles* students are pretty much the same all over the world. The language may change, but the love and peace are always apparent. In Paris, we made friends with a wonderful *Course* teacher named Sylvain, and he and his friend Caroline showed us all over the city. Sylvain has a parking permit, which isn't easy to obtain, so we had a big advantage. During our three visits there in a space of four years, I managed to get Cindy to come to the top of the Eiffel Tower with me. Cindy isn't fond of heights like I am, but she prac-ticed forgiveness and did fine. We visited the Rodin Museum, cruised the River Seine, went to the Louvre, enjoyed the show at the Moulin Rouge, climbed to the top of the Arc de Triomphe, visited Versailles and admired the wonderful fountains, and dined on the Champs-Élysées. I expected the city to be interesting; I didn't expect it to be breathtaking. You can't turn around in Paris without seeing something amazing. Were we glorifying illusions, or were we just being normal? The answer always lies in whether or not you are making it real. Of course if you're making it real and having a good time, you can always remember to forgive it later. That's not a heavy forgiveness lesson; it's one of the easiest. All you have to do is notice it, when you remember to, and then replace it in your mind with the truth.

The answer always lies in whether or not you are making it real.

One of the most fascinating experiences I had in Paris was viewing the *Mona Lisa* when we were at the Louvre. After waiting in the long line, we finally got close to the painting, which is encased in bulletproof glass. The *Mona Lisa* had never seemed like an important painting to me, despite its reputation. When I saw pictures of it in books, I thought it was just a nice, subtle painting of an enigmatic woman. In person, however, it was a different story. I was stunned when I saw the details of the woman's face. I realized what da Vinci had done: he had painted the face of an enlightened person. The gentle smile that the *Course* talks about was captured perfectly, the translucent eyes unmistakable. I got shivers up my spine as I realized that da Vinci himself must have been enlightened. How else could he have known how to produce this image? And was it in a way a self-portrait? Had he disguised himself as a woman? Whether he did or not, the painting was now a great and unusual accomplishment in my mind.

On Saturday, July 7, 2007—that's 07-07-07—Las Vegas broke the record for the most weddings ever held there. Cindy and I were in town just to have a good time. Every now and then, you have a day that goes perfectly. No matter what you do, it works. We went on a phenomenal helicopter tour of the Vegas Strip and the western side of the Grand Canyon, even landing in the canyon to have a picnic overlooking the Colorado River. It was 118 degrees, but we didn't care. When we returned it was still light out, but getting dark. The Strip was lit up, and it was beautiful. It seemed like a happy dream.

With a bride on every corner, we made our way to the Palms Hotel and the Ghostbar, which has one of the best views in Vegas. There was a wedding going on out on the balcony. We weren't invited, but the father of the bride asked us to join them anyway, and we became part of the wedding. It was a joyous occasion.

When it was time for dinner, we decided to go upstairs to a French restaurant called Alizé, which you're supposed to make reservations for way in advance. We didn't think we'd get in, but we gave it a shot. We asked for a table, and there was one left. We were escorted to it like VIPs and had a wonderful dinner. I don't gamble; I don't even know how. But if I had gambled that night, I think I probably would have won.

A lot of the forgiveness lessons that presented themselves during our escapades were found in the effort it took to get from one place to another. Travel can be challenging enough, but when you have a time that you have to be someplace, it makes it more difficult. In my case, if you don't make a connection and get caught up in the system, you may not make the workshop. I would sometimes find myself hurrying through an airport trying to catch a flight and thinking how disappointed the people would be if we didn't show up. Then I'd think of a drawing we had of J on our living-room wall. He was laughing—the way J did 2,000 years ago—and in the caption on the bottom, J was saying, "You're afraid of *what?*" I always smiled when I thought of that, no matter where I was or what I was doing, even rushing through an airport. That's the Holy Spirit at work.

Once we arrived at our destination, it was always rewarding. Yes, doing all-day workshops took just that, work, but because I connected with the Holy Spirit and picked up the energy of the participants, I often felt better at the end of the day than I had at the beginning. I'm not a morning person, but this was worth getting up for.

As the illusion of time went on, Cindy started to participate more in my workshops. At the beginning of 2010 we started playing music together, three or four songs that we spaced out over the course of the day. Cindy had already recorded her second music CD, and we recorded our own together that year. We also did a meditation CD in 2012. I hadn't been in a recording studio since the '80s. It was enjoyable, and also pretty cool to learn new tricks. Cindy was at the top of her game, and she felt very comfortable in that environment. I had to forgive the process, and it took me several sessions to get in my groove. I didn't want to do music for a living again, but I rediscovered the reason I got into music in the first place. It was fun.

Cindy, who had gotten her bachelor's in psychology from California State University, Northridge, decided to attend the University of Santa Monica (USM) and pursue a master's degree in Spiritual Psychology. USM is one of the few places—maybe the only place—in the world where you can get an accredited degree of that kind. Founded by John-Roger, the university has been run and the courses taught by Drs. Ron and Mary Hulnick for over 30 years. Ron and Mary are excellent professors, and I eventually introduced them to my publisher Hay House, who published their first book, *Loyalty to Your Soul: The Heart of Spiritual Psychology.*

In April of 2009, Cindy was working as the receptionist at National Lampoon on Sunset Strip in Hollywood. She enjoyed working there and meeting all kinds of interesting people, including movie stars. Cindy herself had been on television many times doing extra work and getting featured spots on shows like *Married . . . with Children* and *Boy Meets World.* She also did a Christmas video for National Lampoon that was seen by over a million people. She continued extra work and appeared on the TBS series the *Wedding Band* in 2013.

When I got divorced, I had no intention of getting married again anytime soon. There are many people who say they don't intend to get married, or get married again. But then you meet the right person, and it changes everything. I asked the Holy Spirit for guidance, and the guidance I received felt right. I asked Cindy to marry me. We saw no reason to wait, and decided to get married that summer in 2009, on 7/11.

I also told Cindy she could quit her day job if she wanted to and find the best way to use her musical and spiritual talent. After she graduated from USM, she would soon be traveling to almost all of my workshops to do music. She also eventually began to speak more and interact with the audiences along with me. It was a good mix of masculine and feminine energy, and people liked it. I still did most of the teaching, but Cindy added a nice touch. She was no beginner. She was a very advanced spiritual being, a trained and experienced counselor and spiritual advisor, and a knowledgeable practitioner of the *Course.*

Our wedding was in Hawaii, and it was an intimate gathering of close friends and family, held at a beautiful place on the windward side of Oahu called Haiku Gardens. The wedding ceremony was performed by our friends and my split, Michael Tamura, and his wife, Raphaelle. With all the excitement of planning and greeting everyone, Cindy and I realized on the morning of the wedding that we had forgotten to get a marriage license. Fortunately, our friends Jerry and Rochelle were there and drove us around Honolulu, trying to find someone who could give us the license. The courthouse was closed, but we somehow found a justice of the peace who was able to do the job.

Cindy and I decided that we would sing to each other, but not reveal what song we picked so we could make it a surprise. She sang "The First Time Ever I Saw Your Face," and I sang and played the guitar on "When I'm Sixty-Four." Cindy was so emotional she could barely get the words out. She and I hadn't performed together in public yet, so for me it was the first time in almost 20 years. I was really rusty, but we were both able to express ourselves musically during the wedding, which was what we wanted.

It was a beautiful ceremony and reception, held outside in paradise. Cindy and I had spent a five-day honeymoon on the striking and mystical Island of Kauai *before* the wedding, and afterward we spent a few days at Turtle Bay on the North Shore of Oahu.

On Kauai, we visited a gorgeous place called Smith's Tropical Paradise. When we were there, I saw firsthand what a rapport Cindy had with animals. At one point, in one of the lovely gardens, there was a peacock about 30 feet away from us. Cindy started to gently sing "Amazing Grace" to it. At first the peacock cocked its head in the air, seemingly surprised by the pretty sound. Then it slowly turned around and started to tentatively walk toward Cindy, one step at a time in the direction of where the sound was coming from. As Cindy sang, the peacock kept taking small steps toward her until it was right in front of her, listening to the sound as if fascinated, and looking directly at her face.

That was just the first of many times that I saw the effect Cindy could have on animals. We loved to swim with dolphins, and did on a couple of occasions. We swam with bottle-nosed dolphins in captivity on Oahu, and spinner dolphins in the wild at the Big Island. When I was in the water on Oahu with these amazing creatures, I didn't get the impression that I was the smartest being in the water. Hawaiians believe that dolphins can read your thoughts, and I saw no reason to doubt that. The dolphins were so fast and so smart, and they loved to ham it up for the cameras. They got better health care than most people, and were each fed about 18 pounds of fish a day. They were well rewarded for their showmanship, and seemed to be having a good time.

One day we were at the Kahala Hotel, where you can swim with and watch the dolphins, and we were standing on a little bridge that goes over the water. The dolphins were scattered. Cindy held up her hand and said to them, "Show me your beauty." One of the dolphins swam up to where we were standing on the bridge and seemed to be smiling as it played with Cindy, gently spewing little bursts of water right up to Cindy's nose. Then, the other three dolphins swam over and formed a pod—all four of them looking up to Cindy and treating her like a princess. Suddenly, a man started walking over to where we were, and when he got there, all four of the dolphins took off immediately. I guess they didn't like what was in his mind.

On the Big Island, we went out to swim with the dolphins in the wild. China Mike is a legend among those who know dolphins, and the dolphins know him. He's named many of them and recognizes them by the markings and dents on their bodies. We went out with him on a beautiful day to snorkel with the spinners.

Dolphins have three periods of the day. They have their work period, which is fishing. The second is the play period, which is filled with constant sex. Dolphins are very social animals and live in groups, but they aren't monogamous. Then the third is the rest period. If they're near an island and not out in the open sea, they'll usually find a bay to rest in, taking it easy by swimming around slowly.

Dolphins are mammals, and they need to come up to the surface and take a breath every few minutes. They can't go to sleep, or else they would drown. So how do they rest? They put one half of their brain to sleep, while the other half remains awake. This enables them to function and even breathe when they need to. After a few hours, they put the other side of their brain to sleep and use the rested one to function, so they can still come to the surface when they have to. I'd like to see a human being try that.

As people we have all kinds of assumptions. Those assumptions are based on beliefs that subtly make everything in the universe real. One of a thousand examples is that we assume a human body is more valuable than an animal body, and that it's more important to be a person. Yet if bodies are not real, then it can't be more important to have one kind of a body rather than another. Animals can think. Indeed, one of the best things about the Internet, and sites like YouTube, is that you can see from some of the videos that animals are much smarter than humans have ever given them credit for. When I was a boy in school, we were taught that animals weren't capable of abstract thought. That's not true. Animals have their own way of learning, and the Holy Spirit will lead them home. Every seemingly separate mind is going home to the same place, but not as the bodies we thought we were.

As humans, getting there means applying the teachings, not just knowing them. Most people don't even know them, but even if you do, it's not what you know—

It's not what you know—it's what you do with what you know.

it's what you do with what you know. It's the application that matters, which is why the mind-training aspect of the *Course* is paramount. Without applying it, it's just another theory. As the *Course* itself says, "This is not a course in philosophical speculation, nor is it concerned with precise terminology. It is concerned only with Atonement, or the correction of perception. The means of the Atonement is forgiveness."[4] Without utilizing the means, there would be no end to the ego.

Once I was speaking at one of those body, mind, and spirit conferences—this one in London—that make the whole thing real, and I gave the people the teachings straight, as usual. During the break, a tough-looking guy walked up to me, visibly angry. He said, "You keep talking and talking! I'm sick of it. I already know this stuff!" I practiced forgiveness. Not intimidated by his tough-guy routine, I looked him right in the eyes and said, "If you already knew this stuff, you wouldn't be angry." I knew he wanted to hit me, but he didn't. That wouldn't have been very good for his reputation at a body, mind, and spirit conference! So he walked away, unhappy. He wasn't applying the teachings, so they couldn't work for him.

This is why I tell people not to wait to practice forgiveness. Don't wait until next year. Don't wait until your next lifetime. The Song of Prayer section in the *Course* promises that if there has been true healing, which there would be by definition if you've been practicing true forgiveness, then even the experience of death will be a more beautiful one. When you appear to leave the body, you will be prepared for a wonderful experience of liberty.[5]

After the wedding, I was looking forward to seeing Arten and Pursah again. I never really knew what they were going to communicate, but it was always helpful to me. I would have cherished their company and counsel even if no one ever read the books. People forget it was ten years between the time they first appeared to me in Maine, and the time when the first book was ready to be published. There are some who think I did the book for the money. What they fail to realize is that during that entire decade, living in the obscurity of the New England countryside, I had absolutely no guarantee whatsoever that the book would ever be published. What if my teachers were appearing just for me, because that was the form I was ready for? For all I knew, the book could have ended up sitting on my shelf for the rest of my life, another opportunity for forgiveness. And I still would have been very happy that I did it. It was a labor of love.

After I moved to SoCal, I'd occasionally check the weather on my computer to compare the weather in the state I had left with the weather in the state I now lived in. One winter afternoon, when it was 68 degrees in sunny Southern California, and 6 degrees in the gray of Maine, my ascended teachers were back in my living room.

ARTEN: Hey, brother, congratulations! We were there at the wedding. We didn't show ourselves because we didn't want to take away from your day. It was a beautiful location and ceremony. Good for you. You deserve it.

GARY: Thanks, man. I really appreciate you guys being there. I felt your presence, and I often feel your presence at other places, too, especially when I'm doing a radio interview or a workshop.

PURSAH: Yes, we're there. As you know, we're actually the Holy Spirit. When we don't take on a human form, we still often take on a form to communicate with you, which usually comes to you as a Voice or an idea. And let me add my congratulations. I hope you're up for it, buddy. Cindy is 20 years younger than you.

GARY: Nineteen and a half.

ARTEN: We like the way the workshops are going. Have you noticed the difference in the makeup of your audiences over the years?

GARY: I sure have. When I started, ten years ago, it was like 90 percent women. That's cool, but as D.U. has spread, I've seen the percentage of men grow. It's usually around 40 percent now. That's awesome. Our books obviously speak to men as well as women. Plus there are more couples. Partners are sharing the books with each other and starting the *Course,* or coming back to it.

Younger people are also coming. When I started there were mostly older students who were into the *Course* and had been for a while. But that's really changed. Yeah, I still get the seniors, who are becoming ageless in their minds, but I've seen more college people, even teenagers. The population's mind-set is changing. These kids grow up on movies like *The Matrix* and the holodeck on *Star Trek*. The idea that what they're seeing isn't real is a little easier for them to take than the previous generation. Then they read D.U., and they get it. Now I'm speaking to people of all ages.

ARTEN: Very good. That's one of the reasons we came to you—to share the message with people who wouldn't necessarily pick up the *Course* and read it, but we knew would be ready for it if they first heard a linear presentation of it in the vernacular. Then they can pick up the *Course* and apply it sooner than they would have, giving them more time to undo the ego. Of course people can start at any age, and the interlocking chain of forgiveness that the *Course* talks about includes all ages. Then there's the celestial speed up.

GARY: I've meant to ask you about that. What is it?

PURSAH: It's called the celestial speed up because everything that happens on Earth correlates to the movements of the celestial bodies throughout the universe, and your solar system, which in turn correlate to the script. The illusory population is starting to learn the truth faster, although you won't see it on the TV news much. They still make fun of anything that isn't mainstream religion. But it really started with the printing press.

GARY: The printing press?

PURSAH: You've got to remember that people weren't allowed to read scripture for most of history. The clergy—rabbis, priests, and such—could do so, but laymen weren't welcome. How can people decide what they want to believe or not believe when they're not even allowed to see it? With the invention of the printing press, however, all that started to change—not quickly but gradually. It wasn't until the 1700s that you even had enough people who could read for it to make a difference in society.

You didn't have Freud or Jung until a hundred years ago. They opened up a new understanding of the mind and how it works, making an understanding of J's *Course* possible later. Then there was the discovery of the Nag Hammadi Library in Egypt, with its lost gospels. Even though they weren't translated into English until the '70s, they gave people a new, alternate view of J. Now they had a glimpse of J as the enlightened wisdom teacher, instead of the suffering bastard they grew up on. And then there was quantum physics. It came into its own in the first half of the 20th century but wasn't popularized until the '70s.

GARY: Yeah, I remember when I got into est in '78. I take it that's when the speed up really started to accelerate. All of a sudden, people were getting excited about all these ideas. You had Eastern disciplines getting integrated into the West. There was a big group who was interested in enlightenment instead of religion. Dan Millman's *Way of the Peaceful Warrior* intrigued people. Good movie, too, by the way. It took them 30 years to get it made. The movie is just called *Peaceful Warrior.* Nick Nolte wanted to play the young Dan Millman character, but he ended up playing the older guy, the teacher Socrates. He nailed it though. And also quantum physics was being popularized by Gary Zukav's book *The Dancing Wu Li Masters.* I remember listening to the audio book. In addition, est spread fast until '87, when Werner sold it. Eventually it evolved, or devolved, depending on how you look at it, into a gentler version called Landmark. I've heard it's still helpful to people.

PURSAH: Don't forget that in 1965 the Pope allowed Catholics, including the Vatican scholars, to study the Gospel of Thomas and the other lost gospels. J started dictating the *Course* to Helen the same year. People were almost ready. As you know, ideas come out of the unconscious and rise to the surface when enough individuals are ready for them. Today, 85 percent of people describe themselves as spiritual, not religious, even those who go to church. They realize that their relationship with God, or whatever you want to call it, is a personal thing.

By the way, some folks don't like to use the word *God.* But that's because they have an issue with God that they need to forgive. You're not going to undo the idea of separation from God without acknowledging God.

GARY: Also, God is not a he or a she. Technically, God is an It. But that doesn't sound too good. Anyway, when the *Course* uses the word *He* for God, Christ, or the Holy Spirit, it serves as a metaphor. As both the Gospel of Thomas and the *Course* clearly teach, there is no male or female in spirit because there are no differences, opposites, or counterparts. There is only perfect oneness.

ARTEN: Very good. So the *Course* was published in 1976. Today, some will ask you why J didn't give the *Course* and correct Christianity sooner. But the reason he waited was because people could not have understood his teachings on as deep a level as they can now, because all of the things we just talked about had not been disseminated yet. Even today most people don't get it, but more are learning, and the more who learn the faster the speed up becomes. That's because they share the truth with others, either by practicing it silently and influencing other minds, by teaching it in a traditional manner, or doing both like you. Part of the beauty of it is that nobody *has* to do anything. The mind is waking up, and the way that plays itself out is just the effect.

There is no male or female in spirit.

GARY: But not everybody is ready for the *Course*.

PURSAH: That's right. The people who get spirituality the most have always been the poets and other artists. Rumi, Goethe, people who are capable of grasping these grand, abstract ideas. The *Course* speaks on a much bigger level than most people realize at first. Yes, the application is done by a seeming individual, but the men and women who get it have to realize that there's no such thing as an individual, except in a dream. That's why artists, musicians, writers, or those who would like to be often do well with the *Course*. Then, as always, there are exceptions. Einstein was a scientist and could think like one. But he also had the mind of an artist. He loved music, and he could think in abstract terms like no other, understanding and communicating them to people who were ready to expand their awareness.

GARY: Speaking of the celestial speed up, you once told me that someday there would be a President who was capable of hearing the Holy Spirit and would change things a great deal. Is Obama that President?

PURSAH: No. Obama is a good man, but he's not the one we spoke of.

GARY: I see. Well, I like him and his family. I voted for him. People think I'm a Democrat, but I'm really an Independent. I think it's great he's trying to offer affordable health care to everyone, yet some call him a socialist because of that. But America is the only major, industrialized nation in the world that doesn't do that. So does that mean that until now the whole world practiced socialism except for us?

PURSAH: I take it that's a rhetorical question. It's ironic that your health-care system will save countless billions of dollars by insuring everyone. What is universal health care? It's practical. It's also humanistic. People should forgive and get over it.

GARY: You know it's funny. I should have been a lot more excited when Obama got elected. I was happy for him and his family, and I thought it was cool that a black guy got elected President. I think it's about time for a woman, too. But I guess it's because I just wasn't as interested in politics as I used to be. I think there are two reasons. First, I'm not making it real like I used to. Second, I guess that even though I was happy about the election result, I didn't really expect things to change. The deck is too stacked. There would have to be an enormous revolution to change the way the world is run behind the scenes in order for there to be any real, genuine change.

ARTEN: I see that on the level of form you were influenced by that movie.

NOTE: Shortly before this conversation, I'd seen a fascinating film called *Thrive,* which is available online. The film was made by an extremely wealthy whistle-blower, a man who is one of the "haves," not one of the "have-nots." This gave the film more credibility. After seeing it, I thought it could be dangerous for this person to reveal all of these behind-the-scenes secrets to the public, but I admired his courage and commitment.

GARY: Yeah, great movie. The guy is probably dead meat. But you never know; he might luck out. It could be too obvious to snuff him.

ARTEN: Let's talk briefly about Cindy, who was Thaddaeus and will be me in the Windy City. Thaddaeus was a singer, like Cindy, and a drummer, also like her. He had other musical abilities, like Cindy, and shared some of the same forgiveness lessons she is confronted with.

GARY: For instance?

ARTEN: We don't want to invade Cindy's privacy when it comes to her forgiveness lessons. Besides, she may want to speak or write about them in the future. But one of the challenges we had when she and I were Thaddaeus was an issue with anxiety. With Thaddaeus it showed up in two areas: performing in public and being alone with a love interest. That's not how it shows up for Cindy. For her, it shows up in crowded areas. She's already learning to practice true forgiveness with that, and unlike Thaddaeus, who passed away just a few years after Thomas, she will successfully complete that forgiveness lesson in this lifetime.

GARY: Awesome! Can I tell her?

ARTEN: She's going to read this book, isn't she?

GARY: Oh, yeah.

PURSAH: Are you sure you've got what it takes to write this thing?

GARY: Absolutely. I'm an idiot savant.

PURSAH: Good. You had me worried for a minute there. Just kidding, we don't worry.

ARTEN: You and Cindy should both be encouraged. First, you don't have much to forgive about each other in this lifetime. As we said earlier, when some things do show up that need to be forgiven, now you both know what they're for and you both know how to do it. That will pave the way for your final lifetime together, as us. Your final lessons will take place there, and we'll be telling you a little about them. We also want to talk more about the teachings with you. You're doing well, even when you don't feel it.

GARY: Sometimes I just feel like I'm forgiving the same things, over and over again.

PURSAH: That's a common experience with the *Course,* and that's when you need to trust the Holy Spirit. It may look like the same lesson, but it's not the same guilt. Every single time you do this, the Holy Spirit is performing a healing and removing *new* unconscious guilt that is rising to the surface for the first time. This guilt is being healed at the level of the unconscious mind. You can't see it, but there are no exceptions. Remember, even when you think nothing is happening, a miracle is never lost.[6]

You've got to remember that every phase you go through with the *Course* is temporary. Your moods will swing as the ego tries to defend itself, but the ego cannot prevail against the Holy Spirit, and its attacks will eventually wither and die. It's a done deal.

GARY: Oh! Last time I thought you said it's a dumb deal.

PURSAH: Be nice, or we'll bring in Steve. Just kidding again.

NOTE: The first few years I was in California, Cindy and I "accidentally" ran into her former husband, Steve, four times. He wasn't stalking her. He was already at some of the places when we bumped into him. Obviously, we were all in each other's orbits. One of the times we saw Steve we were in San Francisco, hundreds of miles away from home. A person at the front desk of the hotel we were staying at recommended a nice Italian restaurant around the corner. We made a reservation and got a good table at the window.

About halfway through our meal, Cindy said, "Steve's here!" I said, "You've got to be kidding me." She ran out to say hello, and then so did I. I couldn't believe we were running into him again, this time hundreds of miles away from the first couple of times I met him. And the woman he was with probably couldn't believe they were running into Cindy. Steve and I always had brief, but pleasant exchanges.

GARY: He's a good guy. We don't seem to have any issues with each other.

PURSAH: That's true. And he's a pretty open-minded man. He's making progress, too.

GARY: Beautiful. Hey! I've got an *A Course in Miracles* joke for you, and there aren't many *Course* jokes yet, you know.

ARTEN: Well, make it good, and make it fast. We have reservations on Venus.

GARY: All my work is good. I have to maintain certain standards. I have a reputation to live down.

PURSAH: Then proceed, by all means.

GARY: Okay. These three guys are in hell. They're not doing anything special; they're just burning away. And one of them says, "Hey, it looks like we're going to be here for a while. Maybe we should introduce ourselves." They all think that's a pretty good idea.

So the first guy who just spoke says, "Hi. My name is Jacob, and I'm a rabbi. And I'm here in hell because I cheated on my wife."

The second guy says, "That's interesting. My name is Bill, and I'm a Catholic priest, and I'm here in hell because I have a wife."

And the third guy says, "Hi. My name is Joe, and I'm *A Course in Miracles* student, and I'm not here."

PURSAH: Good one. You are redeemed.

ARTEN: I was just kidding about Venus, but we're going to leave. Be good.

GARY: I'll do my best. Say, I was reading this quote this morning from the Workbook. Is it okay if I read it for us before you take your leave?

ARTEN: Always happy to hear from the J guy. And even though you've seen all of these quotes before, you keep getting them on deeper levels. It's not that the words have changed, but you have. As the ego is undone, you are seeing and feeling the words of the quotes from a different place.

GARY: Cool, and thanks. This has to do with what you were saying earlier about trusting the Holy Spirit. There's a lot about the development of trust in the Manual, but this is from the Workbook:

The miracle is taken first on faith, because to ask for it implies the mind has been made ready to conceive of what it cannot see and does not understand. Yet faith will bring its witnesses to show that what it rested on is really there. And thus the miracle will justify your faith in it, and show it rested on a world more real than what you saw before; a world redeemed from what you thought was there.[7]

8

THE FINAL LESSONS OF PURSAH

It is perfectly obvious that if the Holy Spirit looks with love on all He perceives, He looks with love on you. His evaluation of you is based on His knowledge of what you are, and so He evaluates you truly. And this evaluation must be in your mind, because He is.[1]

In this illusory world, you never know where forgiveness, and the Holy Spirit, will lead you. The process can result in unpredictable resolutions of conflict that no one could have dreamed would be resolved. It can lead to meetings with many people who will become part of your life, and they may help you accomplish things for the greater good—not because they have to, but just because they want to. And because you have been prepared to listen, through the grace of the Holy Spirit, you may be led to a fork in the path that, taken the right way, will contribute to the healing of the mind and the salvation of humanity. And of course, there are the everyday situations in your life that humanity doesn't care about, which if forgiven, will bring you peace.

When Karen moved to Oahu in January of 2008, she started dating a nice Japanese gentleman named David Tasaka. They'd met because of me—the connections don't stop. My booking agent, Jan, would occasionally arrange workshops for me in Hawaii, and I did a couple of them at Diamond Head Unity Church.

David, a *Course* student, came to one of the workshops and tagged along with Karen and me and some of the other participants when we went out to dinner afterward. The seed had been planted, and when Karen moved to Oahu, she and David began to see each other. They became a steady item.

When the divorce was final, Karen and I stayed in communication. Our relationship was evolving into becoming good friends, but she didn't talk to Cindy, and I really didn't expect her to anytime soon. Karen didn't know the details about Cindy and me, and it would have been a bit much to expect her to reach out to Cindy, or Cindy to her. But the four of us were all students of the *Course,* and forgiveness is the home of miracles, because the miracle is forgiveness.

A few years after I had been living in California, I received an e-mail from Karen. She and David were coming to the mainland. After visiting her family in Maine, they would go to Florida, where David was a finalist in the Toastmaster speech competition. Then they would head to California, in Orange County, for a little while before flying back to Hawaii. Karen asked if Cindy and I would like to get together and have lunch.

I was surprised and delighted. I had to make sure it was okay with Cindy, and she said yes, absolutely. On a warm summer day, we met Karen and David at a local Olive Garden that was halfway from where they were staying and where we lived. We all said hello, hugged each other, and took a seat. Karen was a little tentative at first with Cindy, but amazingly, within ten minutes or so they were talking with each other as if they were old friends. I had no problem talking with David. He has a great personality and reminded me of my friend Michael Tamura, not because they're both Japanese, but because of the bright smile that David and Michael both seem to be wearing almost all of the time.

As we sat there, I looked to my left and watched Cindy and Karen, who were facing each other, talking across the table. It was too much. I thought to myself, *Oh my God, this forgiveness stuff really works.* This was a scene I didn't know if I would ever see, but here we all were, four *Course* students who knew what it was all for. I was overwhelmed with gratitude.

All I ever really wanted for Karen was for her to be happy, and I think that's what she wants for me. That's also what I want for Cindy, and for David as well. I thought:

May the Holy Spirit lead us all, with God's speed, to the home
We have never really left, but that we are destined to awaken to.

And all God wants is for His Son to be happy. God is perfect Love. Even Saint Paul and the Book of John said that. And there's a quiet revolution taking place within Christianity on the subject, as reported by *Newsweek* magazine in December of 2007 in an article titled "Moderates Storm the Religious Battlefield."

All God wants is for His Son to be happy.

The article from *Newsweek* was sent to me by Rogier Fentener van Vlissingen, the author of *Closing the Circle: Pursah's Gospel of Thomas and A Course in Miracles.* In his book, Rogier demonstrated how D.U. is the bridge between the Thomas Gospel and the *Course.* He also closely examined Pursah's version of the Gospel, as presented by her in *Your Immortal Reality,* and noted that it made more intuitive sense, and was more consistent, than the version discovered in Nag Hammadi in late 1945. In her version, Pursah eliminated 44 of the sayings, which she says were either severely corrupted or added on by others in the more than hundred years after the Crucifixion and before the date of that manuscript. She also did some trimming and pruning of the remaining logia, and combined two of them, to help illustrate their meaning and how they fit together in a way that makes immediate, obvious sense. What emerges is Pursah's version of a kernel of the Thomas Gospel—one that brings the wisdom teacher J of 2,000 years ago to life, and shows very clearly that his voice was the same one then that we find today in *A Course in Miracles.*

The article in question quoted Bart Ehrman, a prolific Bible scholar known mostly for his work on the historical Jesus. According to *Newsweek,* despite his Christian credentials, Ehrman can no longer believe in the Christian God. An all-loving and all-powerful God, he concluded after years of struggle, would not cause so much suffering. This is an odd problem in theology called theodicy, but Ehrman's book *God's Problem* contains so much earnest humility that he will find sympathetic readers even among believers. "Some people think they know the answers," he writes. "Or they aren't bothered by the questions. I'm not one of those people."

For those who are bothered by the questions, perhaps I can humbly suggest that there *is* a place where they can find the answers. But only the Holy Spirit knows when the time and place are right.

In 2011, I was speaking at the International *A Course in Miracles* Conference in San Francisco. It was my fourth time in a row speaking at this particular biannual conference. The organizers wanted to call it "Listen, Learn, and Do," and when I got there I noticed that many of the participants were asking each other, "What do we do? What do we do?" When I got up to speak to the large group, I couldn't help but remind them: "The *Course* says, 'Forgiveness is my function as the light of the world.'² Well, if forgiveness is your function as the light of the world, what the hell do you think you do?"

I wanted to talk to A&P a little more about their future and final lifetime together in Chicago. They didn't disappoint me. However, on this particular visit, Pursah did all the talking, and Arten sat there quietly, listening intently.

GARY: So, what's the scoop on Chicago? I'm pretty excited about it. For one thing, I get to be a babe. That should be interesting.

PURSAH: It is. But what's more interesting is being enlightened. If there's one lifetime that's worth coming back for, it would be the last one. Not that anything is as good as Heaven, but when you're enlightened, it's as close as you can possibly be to Heaven. You're experiencing it almost all the time. Your body feels so light that it's like being in a dream. You can function here, but it's so easy; it's not like the life in the body most people are used to. I was enlightened for 11 years, longer than most. It doesn't matter how long your enlightenment lasts, whether 11 years or 11 minutes.

Once you're enlightened, you're enlightened, and will remain so, until you gently lay the body aside. When I say gently lay the body aside, that's your experience, because you can't feel any pain. At that point the cause of your death becomes meaningless—like J's on the cross. People assumed it must have been horrible, but for him it was nothing.

GARY: Before we get to the end, I'm curious as to what your life was like.

PURSAH: I'll let you in on some of it, but you'll find out the rest on your own. You already know about the biggest forgiveness lessons you'll face. As for the details of my life with Arten, it was pretty normal. I was highly intelligent, and eventually became a professor of psychology. Your interest in the psychological aspects of the *Course* and the mind are a precursor to that. Both Arten and I were born in Chicago, but we never met until later in life. I was married to a wonderful man for 21 years. He was killed in an accident, and that was my first really big forgiveness lesson. You know that man in this lifetime, except he's not a man this time—she's a woman.

GARY: Can you tell me who it is?

PURSAH: I think it's all right to tell you, especially now that you're divorced. The man that you, as a woman, will be married to in your next and final lifetime is your former wife in this lifetime, Karen.

GARY: You're shitting me.

PURSAH: No. You'll have great experiences together, and your husband, whose name is Benji, will learn everything he needs to know in order to be enlightened the next lifetime after that. But since it all fits together, his accidental death in that lifetime will act as a forgiveness lesson that will help you, as me, to become enlightened at the right time. That right time was decided by us and the Holy Spirit at the point at the *end* of time when it was determined what would be best for everyone.

GARY: Because it all has to fit together.

PURSAH: Precisely.

GARY: Did you have any children?

PURSAH: No. It's not unusual for people who are having their last lifetime, or even the next to last, to not have children. The attraction of producing more bodies has diminished. And I'm certainly not saying enlightened people don't have children; it's just not as common as with other couples. There can always be a good reason for having a child, because that fits into the interlocking chain of forgiveness. It's always a question of what you use it for, and what the child eventually uses it for.

Benji and I were big baseball fans—another continuation of your present lifetime. We loved the Cubs and going to the new stadium.

GARY: Do the Cubs finally win the World Series, like the Red Sox did?

PURSAH: They sure do.

GARY: What year? What year?!

PURSAH: Sorry, Gary. I can't tell you that. If I did, then all these gamblers would be making bets at the beginning of the season in Vegas.

GARY: Oh yeah. What else did you like to do?

PURSAH: Like you, I was a movie fan. I liked any kind of video. There's a voyeuristic quality involved, and that's part of both your personality now and my personality in that lifetime. Benji and I had a great holographic unit at our penthouse.

GARY: Penthouse? You must have had money.

PURSAH: Benji was very lucky because his parents had money. Karma, you know. So I was lucky. I was a smart, beautiful woman, and he loved it. But I want to tell you that movies will be quite different a hundred years from now.

GARY: For the better, I hope.

PURSAH: Yes and no. Technology advances so fast. A hundred years from now you won't just be able to go to the movies, you'll be able to go *in* the movie. They'll be holographic—totally lifelike. You'll be able to meet and interact with people who aren't there, like in your life now, and they will seem completely real to you, right down to the touch. You already have the technology today where you can feel things that aren't there. In the future, you'll have movies that mimic reality so completely that you won't be able to tell the difference between the real illusion and the phony illusion.

GARY: Wow. Can you, like, have sex in the movie and stuff?

PURSAH: Yes, but of course there will be a big moral debate about it. The Christian right will freak, and those kinds of movies won't be available everywhere.

GARY: Imagine the temptation to think you're a body, and to keep coming back for more, so you can act out your fantasies!

PURSAH: Down, boy. Remember something, Gary. If you're a *Course* student, then it doesn't matter if the image you're seeing is one that's in a movie that seems completely real, or one you see in your everyday life that seems completely real. They are both equally forgivable because they are both equally untrue. Even if you forget where you are, all you ever have to do is forgive what's right in front of your face.

All you ever have to do is forgive what's right in front of your face.

GARY: Got it. But I'm still going to the movies as you, right?

PURSAH: Yes. Now, I'm not going to repeat the part of the story I gave you during the first series of visits. You remember it well, and you can always look it up. In D.U. it's on pages 250 to 253 or so. Arten's story from our final lifetime is on pages 294 to 296. That's in English. We know the books are in 22 languages, and other people will have to figure out the page numbers themselves, or at least the translators will have to.

GARY: So in English it's on page 294, and in Spanish it's on page 487.

PURSAH: That's funny. You always have a good time in Mexico and South America, don't you?

GARY: I love it. The people are so warm, they practically adopt you. And places like Rio and Bogotá . . . I'll tell you, they know how to have a good time.

PURSAH: That's an art in itself. So my first big lesson in that lifetime was forgiving the death of Benji. He witnessed an accident and tried to help a person who was trapped in a car. There was water on the ground, and Benji didn't realize that when the car hit a utility pole, a live wire fell in the water. He stepped in the water and was electrocuted.

GARY: Bummer. You must have been devastated.

PURSAH: Yes, I missed him terribly, but I had J and his *Course*, and I forgave everything. It was still a year before I was in a condition of total forgiveness. People should take the time to grieve. There are going to be so many memories in your mind, especially if you had a long relationship, and you need to come to terms with everything. Benji helped me through it. Sometimes he'd come to me in my dreams, and we'd make love.

GARY: Was he really there?

PURSAH: Was he really there before?

GARY: I got it. It's all your projection, although sometimes it can be the Holy Spirit taking on a form. But ultimately, it's a split-off part of yourself. I like what Cindy said about it—that the human race is one great big multiple personality disorder.

PURSAH: She's a smart, beautiful woman, and you love it.

GARY: The way Benji loved you.

PURSAH: The episode at the university—when a disturbed student accused me of propositioning him for sex in order to get a good grade—ruined my career as a professor. That was my second huge lesson. I call that a slow burn, because when something like that happens, it takes place over a long period of time and you have to persevere with forgiveness, over and over, until you get through it. After a couple of years, I made it through. Yes, it sounds hard, but if you do it, you progress so much in your spiritual advancement that you save lifetimes of future learning. I did it.

GARY: So you could say you were able to Pur-sah-vere.

PURSAH: Don't ever say that again. The last two lessons of my life came at once, and they weren't really lessons because I had already attained enlightenment. But I had a part to play in helping Arten attain his. His last huge forgiveness opportunity was the death of my body. My part was seeing him as Christ, even though I could tell he was upset at knowing my body was going to be laid aside. When you see someone with spiritual sight in that situation, it helps teach him or her to do the same in the future. And I wanted to encourage him by assuring him that we would never be apart. We are one. Plus, I wasn't feeling any pain, which made him feel better. I was in a condition of total peace. That last day, I quoted this part of the *Course* to him, which I knew by heart:

> Teacher of God, your one assignment could be stated thus: Accept no compromise in which death plays a part. Do not believe in cruelty, nor let attack conceal the truth from you. What seems to die has but been misperceived and carried to illusion. Now it becomes your task to let the illusion be carried to the truth.[3]

GARY: Sounds like you really had it down.

PURSAH: Decades of practice will do that for you. So, we're going to leave and let you think about this. Arten will do the talking next time. But for now, I'd like to give you the rest of that quotation from the *Course,* for it has great meaning. Be well, dear brother.

> Be steadfast but in this; be not deceived by the "reality" of any changing form. Truth neither moves nor wavers nor sinks down to death and dissolution. And what is the end of death? Nothing but this: the realization that the Son of God is guiltless now and forever. Nothing but this. But do not let yourself forget it is not less than this.[4]

9

THE FINAL LESSONS OF ARTEN

The special relationship has the most imposing and deceptive frame of all the defenses the ego uses. Its thought system is offered here, surrounded by a frame so heavy and so elaborate that the picture is almost obliterated by its imposing structure. Into the frame are woven all sorts of fanciful and fragmented illusions of love, set with dreams of sacrifice and self-aggrandizement, and interlaced with gilded threads of self-destruction. The glitter of blood shines like rubies, and the tears are faceted like diamonds and gleam in the dim light in which the offering is made.

Look at the <u>picture.</u> Do not let the frame distract you. This gift is given for your damnation, and if you take it you will believe that you are damned. You cannot have the frame without the picture. What you value is the frame, for there you see no conflict. Yet the frame is only the wrapping for the gift of conflict. The frame is not the gift. Be not deceived by the most superficial aspects of this thought system, for these aspects enclose the whole, complete in every respect. Death lies in this glittering gift. Let not your gaze dwell on the hypnotic gleaming of the frame. Look at the picture, and realize that death is offered you.

That is why the holy instant is so important in the defense of truth. The truth itself needs no defense, but you do need defense against your acceptance of the gift of death.[1]

Ever since I spoke with Pursah about her final lifetime, I wanted to do the same with Arten. Arten had grown on me. At first I had a natural dislike for him because of his tall, dark, handsome, Greek god–type looks. I was jealous, especially since Pursah had become my fantasy in the 1990s. Because of their reality as ascended masters, this was stupid of me. Sometimes you know something is stupid, and it doesn't stop you. And when you learn the ego thought system is stupid, that doesn't stop you from acting like an ego. It takes a lot of work, and a lot of forgiveness.

By the fall of 2012, almost 20 years since I had first seen my teachers, I had a deep respect for Arten, as well as Pursah, and love for both of them, too.

Also by that year, my life and schedule started to become saner. The IRS tax audit of nearly three years was over. They'd wanted me to pay about $150,000. I ended up paying about $6,000 plus another $5,000 to my excellent CPA for her work during that timeframe. Not bad, considering the ransom the government had initially demanded in order to cease its extortion.

If Pursah was true to her word, and she always was, then Arten would be doing the talking during their next visit. I had a feeling they would be showing up that afternoon because Cindy had a hair appointment, and she would be gone for about four hours. After I moved to California, my teachers came at times when Cindy wasn't home, or they visited me once in a great while in my hotel room on the road if Cindy wasn't with me.

I wondered if they would ever appear to my wife. After all, Arten was Cindy in her next and final lifetime, just as Pursah was me. The only dilemma was a promise they had made around 2004. They said they would appear *only* to me. There was a reason for that, and it wasn't because I'm special. They didn't want the message to be changed.

It would be easy for others to say that Arten and Pursah were appearing to them, and this is what they said. And if they were anything like the channelers who had made up their own versions of the *Course,* then the message would leave out the most important parts and not undo the ego. Indeed, I had met and spoken at the same conferences as some of these people, who were revered by their followers, and even though they occasionally quoted from the *Course* as if they were teaching it, or something like it, I was shocked by their lack of understanding of it and why it worked. Their presentations taught methods that would do nothing except make their practitioners temporarily feel good, inevitably delaying them from the goal of salvation.

An older gentleman in Wisconsin who humbly called himself the "Master Teacher of *A Course in Miracles*," and who had once actually hit me in public, told his followers in 2006 that Arten and Pursah were appearing to him, and that he could communicate their message better than I could. Fortunately, my second book had just been released, and a couple of people told him that Arten and Pursah had said they would definitely not appear to anyone but me. The "master teacher" stopped saying that A&P were visiting him. My teachers knew what they were doing.

In fact, it's partially because of that gentleman why I tell people in no uncertain terms that if a teacher of the *Course* wants you to come and live with them, don't. That's a cult. *A Course in Miracles* is a self-study process, and that is clearly stated right in the Preface: "It is not intended to become the basis for another cult."[2] If someone is setting up a "Course Community"—whether in North America, South America, Denmark, or any place else on Earth—and wants you to come and live with, or near, other *Course* students, don't go. They will make you somehow dependent on the community and perhaps even subtly persuade you to "donate" your money, car, and even your house to them. As the *Course* also says, "Time can waste as well as be wasted."[3] He who has two good ears to hear, let him hear!

That afternoon, with Cindy having a good hair day, Arten and Pursah appeared to me once again.

ARTEN: So, you're looking a little tired today. You should shut off that big-screen TV of yours and get to bed earlier. We want you to be fresh for these discussions.

GARY: It's not my fault. I'm a victim of God.

ARTEN: Oh, I'm sorry. I didn't know. You'd like to hear something about my final lifetime? I think that would be fine.

GARY: Don't you think it would be fair for Cindy to hear this? I mean, after all, you're her. It's her final lifetime, too.

ARTEN: It's not that I don't think she deserves it. As far as that final lifetime is concerned, if she reads this book we're doing, then she'll know just as much about it as you do. But she doesn't need us as much as you used to need us when we first started appearing to you. You're French. She's more independent. She's Swiss.

GARY: Enough with the international stereotypes. Are you saying you'll never appear to her?

ARTEN: Actually, I'm not saying that. We know she can be trusted to not change the message, so you never know. If it happens, it happens. What do you say we move on?

GARY: Fair enough. Pursah here, who is so attractive when she's silent, gave me some of the scoop, so I'm now in the loop. Can't help it; I'm a musician. Would you like to share about Cindy's and my future?

ARTEN: Sure, you musical fool. Pursah, by the way, was not gifted with musical talent in that lifetime. Her focus was on psychology and spirituality. Apparently your musicianship had a falling out with your gene pool. But I, on the other hand, inherited some musical talent from Cindy and Thaddaeus, and I took advantage of it when I was younger. I played the drums in college, and was quite a hit with the sorority girls.

GARY: I knew you were a horn dog. And being a drummer is almost like being a musician. Did drumming come naturally to you, or did you take a lesson?

ARTEN: It came naturally, plus I could sing. As you know, if you can sing, it doubles your importance as a musician. I had Cindy and Thad, as we call him in the business, to thank for that. As I started to get a little older though, my thoughts turned to being a psychiatrist. Not a psychologist, mind you, but an M.D. If I wanted to, I could prescribe medication to my patients.

GARY: There's a lot of money in that. How often did you do it?

ARTEN: Not very much. I wasn't your typical psychiatrist. I wasn't a fan of big pharma. Money is more important to the industry than life is, and cures for diseases have been suppressed. But I was a *Course* student by the time I was 25. As I started to grasp its meaning, I got the idea that I'd try to get my patients to change their thoughts by training their minds, instead of doping them up.

GARY: Wow, buddy. I take back all those things I've been thinking about you that were just screwing me up anyway.

ARTEN: Thank you. Remember, the gifts you give are saved for you.

GARY: Don't paraphrase. So you became a psychiatrist, but you tried to get your patients to change their mind to change their mood, instead of putting them on medication. You said you didn't prescribe drugs much, so did it work?

> **Remember, the gifts you give are saved for you.**

ARTEN: I had as good a success rate as anyone, sometimes better. If a patient was ready for it, I'd turn them on to the *Course*. If not, I'd practice forgiveness on them. I was always very interested in the *Course* extension "Psychotherapy: Purpose, Process and Practice."

GARY: Yeah. I call it the psycho section for short.

ARTEN: Notice that nowhere in that section does J tell the therapist to change his method. What he's doing is advising the therapist to do the job he's been trained to do, and practice forgiveness at the same time. In that sense, as you read through it, whenever you see the word *therapist,* you could simply substitute the name of whatever your job is, and it would still work.

I used the *Course*, forgiveness, and for those who weren't ready for the *Course* but could tolerate a secular-sounding discipline instead, I helped them with a mind-training program that would change their thoughts. As you know, you can heal a majority of the depression in the world if you could train people to get a hold of the power of their mind and stop thinking the garbage they've been hanging on to their whole lives about other people, as well as themselves. You've got to break the pattern of thought and give them something to replace it with.

I have to give Cindy some of the credit for my ability to do that work. She's becoming a great therapist, which is a gift that will carry over into her next lifetime.

GARY: Very cool. Hey, people ask me about that Ho'oponopono forgiveness method. Did you use that?

ARTEN: No. It doesn't go all the way. Plus, I didn't like the "I'm sorry" part.

GARY: So this is in the future. Did your method catch on?

ARTEN: It started to. I had the impression I may have started a trend. I published some papers, and they were moderately read, like your books.

GARY: Funny. Anyway, I think it's great that you did that. So what were the other parts of your life like, and how did you attain enlightenment?

ARTEN: I was married by the time I was 30. I wouldn't meet Pursah until I was in my early 60s. Being 60 a hundred years from now is like being 40 today. It's very normal for people to live to be 120 years old at the turn of the next century. The average life span is 100. It's also not that unusual for people to be married three or four times in a lifetime. But Pursah and I were monogamists from the time we each got married to other people, me in my 30s and her in her 40s.

GARY: And whom were *you* married to? I'm afraid I might know the answer to that, given the person that Pursah was married to.

ARTEN: You got it, bright student. Steve, who was Cindy's, or my, first husband in the previous lifetime, was a woman, and my wife, in that next and final lifetime. So you see, trials really *are* lessons presented once again. Not that we had a lot of lessons; in fact, we got along fine. I would have been happy with Charlene—that was her name—the rest of my life. Even a couple of years after she passed away, I had no intention of getting married again.

GARY: Any children?

ARTEN: No. I hate kids, the little bastards. Just kidding. It was a similar story to Pursah's. We met when we were supposed to, and knew within two days we'd probably be spending the rest of our lives together.

GARY: Excellent. And I know you love everybody, including children and animals.

ARTEN: They're actually the easiest to love. In any case, aside from the times I'd turn some of my patients on to the *Course,* I didn't teach it in that lifetime, and neither did Pursah. At least we didn't teach it in the traditional sense. We lived it. As the *Course* says:

> To teach is to demonstrate. There are only two thought systems, and you demonstrate that you believe one or the other is true all the time. From your demonstration others learn, and so do you.[4]

We didn't take on a traditional teaching role like you did. You were guided to do that because it would be helpful. But you also demonstrate with your forgiveness.

GARY: I'm a double threat. That's why I make the big bucks, and you don't.

ARTEN: Where I live, you don't need money. And your time is coming. Then there will be no time.

Charlene made her transition when I was 52. She was walking to the store to buy some food. There was a gang fight, and she got hit with a stray bullet in the head. I thought I'd die when I heard the news, but I didn't. I had cherished our time together and felt like my life was over, *Course* or no *Course.* I slowly forgave, and tried to learn to live again, but my heart wasn't in it.

But then I met Pursah when I was in my 60s, and she made everything new again. We started with a special love relationship, but within months, it was a holy relationship. She was enlightened about eight years later. We both knew it. But nobody would know it if they saw us on the sidewalk or in a restaurant. The only difference others would notice is that Pursah smiled more frequently than most people, as the *Course* says.

That's when we started to do mind transport, about a year after she was enlightened. My mind wasn't quite as powerful as hers, but we knew I was getting there. When your awareness increases, because the ego interference has been completely undone, your mind can do anything. We tried not to be too obvious about it. We'd mostly zap ourselves off to places where there weren't any people. When your unconscious mind has been completely healed by the Holy Spirit, there are no blocks or barriers; there's nothing to hold you back. You just think and you're there. At first, I couldn't have done it without joining with Pursah's mind. When we transported *you,* we had already joined our minds with yours.

We also did some levitation, but I thought the mind transport was more fun. Then, of course, you realize every place is the same, which you already knew, but it's another confirmation of your new perception. You never really *go* anywhere. It's all a projection.

Eventually, after Pursah's transition, I became enlightened. It was because of her that I had been able to truly forgive and learn my final lesson, the passing of her body. She did a great job coaching me during her transition. Now we're manifestations of the Holy Spirit. Our images are used to teach, not for anything else. When we're not communicating with you, we are home in God. It's a glorious existence, Gary. No such thing as lack or problems or death or loneliness. There's such a fullness and a wholeness. It's complete. And the love is almost too much! Your cup really does runneth over. If you knew the joy that awaits you, you'd be jumping up and down right now.

When you and Cindy live that final lifetime, you'll remember just enough as Pursah and Arten to put the pieces of the puzzle together from your previous lifetime, and also the final one. But you'll *forget* just enough so that you can still have the few forgiveness lessons that you need to be enlightened. That's why the Holy Spirit chose that time for you to be released to revelation and eternity.

It's been a pleasure being with you, brother. Don't tell anyone I told you this, but I like your work. Keep it up. We're going to leave you today, as we often do, with a wonderful quote from our leader. We will always be his disciples for teaching purposes, even though we are one with him in Heaven. God bless, and Godspeed.

GARY: Thanks so much, guys. I love you.

ARTEN: We love you, too, Gary. By the way, the first line in this quote refers to the body:

The branch that bears no fruit will be cut off and will wither away. Be glad! The light will shine from the true Foundation of life, and your own thought system will stand corrected. It cannot stand otherwise. You who fear salvation are choosing death. Life and death, light and darkness, knowledge and perception, are irreconcilable. To believe that they can be reconciled is to believe that God and his Son can *not*. Only the oneness of knowledge is free of conflict. Your kingdom is not of this world because it was given you from beyond this world.[5]

10

LOVE HAS FORGOTTEN NO ONE

We are the bringers of salvation. We accept our part
as saviors of the world, which through our joint forgiveness
is redeemed. And this, our gift, is therefore given us. We look on
everyone as brother, and perceive all things as kindly and
as good. We do not seek a function that is past the gate of
Heaven. Knowledge will return when we have done our part.
We are concerned only with giving welcome to the truth.

Ours are the eyes through which Christ's vision sees a world
redeemed from every thought of sin. Ours are the ears that
hear the Voice for God proclaim the world as sinless. Ours
the minds that join together as we bless the world. And from
the oneness that we have attained we call to our brothers,
asking them to share our peace and consummate our joy.[1]

It's heresy to the ego to think that what you do is not important. *Of course* what I do is important! *Of course* what happens in my life is *very* important! Why? You believe in it. If you didn't believe it, it wouldn't be important.

If a scientist makes a hologram in a laboratory, it can be very impressive and intricate. It can be analyzed and well planned, ready to wow anyone who sees it. Yet there is no image. There's nothing there—nothing to be impressed by and nothing to believe in. It's only when the scientist shines a laser beam through the hologram that it shows up and looks real. Without the power of the laser beam, there's nothing to be wowed by.

The power that lights up the universe of time and space, and makes it seem so real to us is the power of our belief. Of itself, the universe is nothing. It's a projection that is coming from the deep canyons of our own collective, unconscious mind. And we, as one seemingly separate ego mind, are the cause of it. It wasn't a good idea, no more than it was a good idea for the prodigal son in J's profound miscreation story to leave home. In fact, it was a bonehead move. All he found was scarcity. And even if he temporarily got a lot, it still wasn't everything, so it was still scarcity. But there can be no scarcity in perfect oneness, where you have everything by definition. The only logical solution for someone who left home when he shouldn't have is to go back there.

> **There can be no scarcity in perfect oneness, where you have everything by definition.**

Because we believe in this world and think it's the most important part of this universe, for it's all we seem to have, it has power over us. It's our belief that gives it that power and puts us at the effect of it.

If you can learn how to withdraw that belief in the world, and put the belief where it really belongs, you can successfully undo the thought system that gave rise to the belief in the first place. You can return to a condition of cause and change your mind. Then you can, as the *Course* so clearly and succinctly puts it: "Choose once again if you would take your place among the saviors of the world, or would remain in hell, and hold your brothers there."[2]

You make this choice by choosing spiritual sight instead of the ego's "sight." It's done by investing your belief in totally innocent spirit everywhere, instead of in what the body's false eyes appear to be showing you. And so you overlook what you're being shown, and instead think of the truth.

It may be fair for you to ask, "How can I do that, when the world is always in my face?" And that would be a legitimate question. You've been set up by an expert. And from the moment you appear to be born to the moment you appear to die, you will be confronted by an endless series of problems. These problems are designed to distract your attention to the illusory screen you are viewing, hopefully forever, and keep your attention away from the place where the answer to life lies: in the mind that projected the false universe in the first place, and then convinced you it was all true.

It will take vigilance for you to change your mind, but that vigilance is the only thing that will lead you to happiness. There's nothing in this world that will do it. Does that mean you can't have the world? Ironically, you *can* have it. You just can't *believe* in it. That's how you give up the world, and you do have to give it up. But you give it up mentally, not physically, unless you feel guided by the Holy Spirit to do so in order to instill discipline. That's an individual guidance and it is not the same for everyone.

Happiness cannot be dependent upon circumstances. If it is, you're screwed, because the only thing you can count on in a world of shift and change is that it's going to shift and change. If you use the law of attraction and get what you want, which from observation seems to happen for about one in a hundred people who try it, it's still not going to last.

Nothing here is permanent. What has seeming life one moment can be snuffed out the next. That's not meant to discourage you; it's meant to point you to something that can never be altered—something that can make you happy in a permanent way, because it's not dependent on what happens. That's real spirituality, and it can be there for you no matter what appears to happen. And you can still have your life. It's just that now you're looking at it differently, from above the battleground. You're looking at life—and everything and everyone you see—with spiritual sight.

Even practicing the law of attraction, and other popular self-help techniques, would be a totally different experience, and would work a lot more often, if you did it with the Holy Spirit. The forgiveness process, which leads to true abundance, is the missing ingredient in these methods. When you work with the Holy Spirit, you're not alone. When you're making decisions, and doing things yourself, that's separation. That's also disaster. "Aster" means astral. *Disaster* means you're not connected to that higher place that knows better. The best way to be connected is to undo the ego interference that separates you from your true being, which is spirit. Then you can be guided to what's best for everyone, instead of what's best for your ego—that thing that wants to convince you that you're a body in order to keep its crazy game of separation going.

With the Holy Spirit, everything you do can be an expression of love. Then it's not what you do that matters—it's the love. If you're coming from a loving place, you're not going to be doing bad things; you're going to be doing good things. The forgiveness that undoes the ego leads to love automatically, because love and spirit are synonymous. Now what's in your mind, which is cause, is love, instead of the ego. Love needs nothing because it already has everything in a condition of oneness with spirit. You don't have to get anything from anybody. You can have a holy relationship. You can come from a place of abundance. How ironic that you are more likely to be led to abundance when you're already there.

Our belief in the universe of time and space needs to be dispelled. In fact, the *Course* uses the word *dispel* 26 times. That belief can be returned to God and His Kingdom if we stop thinking with the ego, start thinking with the Holy Spirit, and see through the eyes of Christ. Will we still be shown bodies by the ego? Yes, until we gently lay our bodies aside for the final time and go home. But we can choose to acknowledge only reality with our belief. As the *Course* tells us, "Salvation does not ask that you behold the spirit and perceive the body not. It merely asks that this should be your choice."[3] Then knowing that as we see him we will see ourselves,[4] it cannot help but dawn upon our mind that we are Christ as one, which is the perfect Love that we truly are.

It was now the first week of January, 2013. I had more questions for Arten and Pursah, and it had been longer than usual since their last appearance. I'd recorded a movie on cable TV that I'd wanted to see for a long time and was just about to watch it when, suddenly, they were with me. They seemed happy, and so was I. Pursah, who hadn't spoken during the last appearance, began the discussion.

PURSAH: Hey buddy, sorry to interrupt you. What were you going to watch?

GARY: It's called *Vampyros Lesbos*.

PURSAH: Well, we're sorry to delay your social explorations, but we'd like to cover a couple of things. Our book project, *Love Has Forgotten No One,* is just about complete. It will also complete the *Disappearance* trilogy.

GARY: Wow. I didn't even think of it as being a trilogy, but I guess it is.

ARTEN: Oh yes. It all fits together like a hologram. You've done well. You took longer than we advised you to on this one, but it turned out that you had a lot of extra lessons, and you were ready for them. Your life will be a little calmer now, which means you'll have more time to write.

GARY: Does that mean we'll do more books together?

PURSAH: That's always up to you and the Holy Spirit, Gary. You know that. You're going to be writing other things, too, though. So we'll leave it like this: If you ever want us to come back and visit you, just ask. We'll hear you, and then we'll choose a time that's best for everyone. No matter what work you do—whether it's with Cindy or anyone else, writing for the screen, whatever—we'll always be here for you *if* you want us to be. Of course you always have our Guidance in your mind, too.

GARY: Great! If I don't see you for a long time, I'll miss you. I mean, I know it's all just images and stuff, but you're my friends.

ARTEN: And you're our friend. We're the *RAP* team.

GARY: And that means?

ARTEN: RAP: Renard, Arten, and Pursah.

GARY: I think you should stick with salvation and leave the promotional aspects of this to me.

ARTEN: I can live with that. Now, we know you have a couple of questions you've been meaning to ask us.

GARY: Yeah. There have been a lot of highly visible tragedies on the news lately, and when I'm at the workshops or on the Internet, people have been asking about the victims. Sure, I tell them to forgive, but do either of you have any more specific advice?

PURSAH: That's always a tough one for most. True forgiveness is *always* the answer. We know you can do it, but for beginners, a tragedy with a lot of victims is difficult to come to terms with. So first, they've got to try to accept that the reason they're feeling bad is because they're looking at the situation with the ego.

ARTEN: Yes. Some people have gotten used to monitoring their thoughts and catching themselves when they're thinking negatively. But as you know, few monitor their feelings. When people are feeling distraught, that's when arguments and violence happen. So you and others have also got to catch yourself as soon as you start to feel bad, judgmental, hurt inside, sorry, or uncomfortable in any way. It could be a subtle feeling or outright anger, but it's all the same, and it's always the ego. And as soon as you notice it, you need to *stop.* You want to stop thinking with the ego. If you're watching TV and see a terrible news story—like a tsunami or an earthquake decimating an area—you need to stop and switch to the Holy Spirit. Think of the Holy Spirit in your mind. That's where the discipline comes in. You've got to do it. That's why the Workbook is so important, as it will help train people's minds to think that way.

PURSAH: Once you're thinking with the Holy Spirit, you can remember that what you're seeing in a tragedy or natural disaster is a trick to perceive the victims as bodies instead of spirit, and thus, think of yourself as a body instead of spirit. But now, because you know better, you can choose the Holy Spirit's miracle instead. J says:

> A miracle is a correction. It does not create, or really change at all.
> It merely looks on devastation, and reminds the mind that what it
> sees is false.[5]

Then you can take the third step and think outside of the system. Think beyond the veil to the truth, and the truth is the Atonement. Do you remember what the full awareness of the Atonement is?

GARY: Sure. Once again, it's that the separation never occurred.[6]

PURSAH: Right, so if the ego's idea of separation never happened, you can choose to *not* believe the ego, believe the Holy Spirit instead, and remember the light of truth that is beyond the veil. As J puts it so strikingly, late in the Text of the *Course:*

> In joyous welcome is my hand outstretched to every brother who would join with me in reaching past temptation, and who looks with fixed determination toward the light that shines beyond in perfect constancy.[7]

GARY: Got it. It takes a lot of determination to do that though.

PURSAH: Yes, you've got to want it.

ARTEN: What does the *Course* say about the words "I want the peace of God"?

GARY: I know. "To say these words is nothing. But to mean these words is everything."[8]

PURSAH: Yes. And there you have it. The truth isn't going to change, Gary. But you must have the willingness to accept it. At first, it's the little willingness to listen to the Holy Spirit. But later, it's the abundant willingness to want the peace of God beyond anything else that appears to exist, and that takes commitment. Are you up for it?

GARY: Yes, more than ever.

PURSAH: I believe you. So do it, and love will be the result.

GARY: I'm experiencing the presence of love more and more. When you used to leave, I'd feel alone—except for a few great experiences I had once in a while, even though you had left. Now I never feel alone. In fact, I know that I *can't* be alone, because the Holy Spirit is always with me.

ARTEN: Excellent. Most people feel lonely from time to time, but just as Thaddaeus told you he was taught by J 2,000 years ago, the truth is they can never be alone.

GARY: That reminds me of a quote I like. Let me grab it.

ARTEN: You're pretty good at finding those things.

GARY: You gave me a lot of practice, especially those first ten years. Here it is. Pursah was just talking about not believing the ego, and here you are, talking about not being alone. This really nails J's attitude about that:

> The whole purpose of this course is to teach you that the ego is un-believable and will forever be unbelievable. You who made the ego by believing the unbelievable cannot make this judgment alone. By accepting the Atonement for yourself, you are deciding against the belief that you can be alone, thus dispelling the idea of separation and affirming your true identification with the whole Kingdom as literally part of you.[9]

GARY: Awesome, eh?

ARTEN: Awesome, bro.

PURSAH: As the ego's blocks are undone, and you grow in your awareness of spirit, love will not just be something that you do—it will be something that you are, which you share with God. It is not arrogant to think you are the same as God. That's simply the truth. What is arrogant is to think that you can be *separate* from God. That is the arrogance of the ego.

Extend your love into the world that isn't there. It doesn't matter that it's an illusion. What matters is the love. You are now God's representative in a strange land, but you will never stop being exactly what He is. The *Course* describes you thus, and there could be no better way to close our quotations from our elder brother.

> Hallowed your name. Your glory undefiled forever. And your whole-ness now complete, as God established it. You are His Son, complet-ing His extension in your own. We practice but an ancient truth we knew before illusion seemed to claim the world. And we remind the world that it is free of all illusions every time we say:
>
> *God is but Love, and therefore so am I.*[10]

GARY: Yes. I love that. Thank you. Thank you forever.

ARTEN: Keep it coming, brother. Keep knockin' 'em alive.

PURSAH: Join with us now. Our bodies will disappear, the world will disappear, and you will be completely spirit. You'll hear the Voice for God for a while and then nothing. The brilliant abstraction of perfect oneness will replace it and give you another taste of what will be yours forever, and that you can never lose. Eventually, you will return to the world of form for a while, but you'll be even more certain of your loving fate. Your mind will feel the glory of your true eternal life, as the Holy Spirit comforts you and cradles you in God.

> *You can only be encouraged, and help your brothers home*
> *You are not feeling weary, for you have feet of wings*
> *You cannot be dispassionate, with fire in your soul*
> *You are not one to judge them, you have a loving heart*
> *You only speak the truth, for spirit is your Voice*
> *You cannot be afraid, for I am here with you*
> *And all is one in Heaven*
> *You have been remembered*
> *For Love has forgotten no one*

INDEX OF REFERENCES

In the following Index, the first numeral listed is the footnote number for the given chapter, followed by the standard designation of the page number of a quoted reference from *A Course in Miracles*. Page numbers refer to the official version published by the Foundation for Inner Peace. *Course* references are signified as follows:

T: Text
W: Workbook for Students
M: Manual for Teachers
CL: Clarification of Terms
P: Psychotherapy: Purpose, Process and Practice
S: The Song of Prayer

All page numbers are for the third edition of the *Course,* printed in 2007 and after, which is exactly the same as the second edition of the *Course,* printed in 1992 and after, except that the Psychotherapy and Song of Prayer pamphlets are included at the end of the third edition because they were also dictated by Jesus to Helen Schucman.

Introduction/Frontispiece/1. What Would You Rather Be?
  1. T176. 2. T38. 3. T667. 4. W13. 5. M15, M13. 6. T142.
  7. W442. 8. T98. 9. W48. 10. W1. 11. T248. 12. W281–282. 13. T45.

14. CL77. 15. T142. 16. W298. 17. T586. 18. T350. 19. T447.
20. Introduction. 21. T307. 22. T327.

2. **A Tour of the In-Between Life.** 1. T344. 2. T59. 3. T666.
4. W58. 5. M61. 6. T388. 7. T445. 8. S17–18. 9. M64.
10. T128. 11. P22. 12. T352. 13. W291. 14. Ibid. 15. T291.
16. T336.

3. **The Script Is Written, but Not Etched in Stone: The Nature of Dimensions.** 1. T335. 2. CL77. 3. T5. 4. T21. 5. Ibid.
6. T11.

4. **Bodily Healing for an Enlightened Mind.** 1. T105. 2. T84.
3. M18. 4. T104. 5. T497. 6. T493. 7. T101–102.

5. **Lessons of Thomas and Thaddaeus.** 1. T37. 2. CL89. 3. T94.
4. T563. 5. T90. 6. T666. 7. S11. 8. T372–373. 9. CL79.
10. W216.

6. **Lessons of Gary.** 1. W73. 2. M7. 3. T5. 4. T6. 5. T473. 6. T5.
7. T29. 8. T109. 9. T568. 10. T475. 11. M11–12. 12. T84.
13. W324. 14. T667. 15. Introduction. 16. T3. 17. W324.
18. Ibid. 19. T303. 20. CL77. 21. W58. 22. W264. 23. T496.
24. T467. 25. Ibid. 26. T667. 27. W473.

7. **Arten in This Lifetime.** 1. M60. 2. M61. 3. M60. 4. M77.
5. S17. 6. T6. 7. W473.

8. **The Final Lessons of Pursah.** 1. T175. 2. W104. 3. M67.
4. Ibid.

9. **The Final Lessons of Arten.** 1. T359–360. 2. Preface viii.
3. T12. 4. M1. 5. T51.

10. **Love Has Forgotten No One.** 1. W479. 2. T666. 3. T661.
4. T142. 5. W473. 6. T98. 7. T668. 8. W348. 9. T131.
10. W331.

ABOUT *A COURSE IN MIRACLES*

The Combined Volume, Third Edition of *A Course in Miracles* is the only edition that contains in one place all the writing that Dr. Helen Schucman, its scribe, authorized to be printed. It is published solely by the Foundation for Inner Peace, the organization chosen by Dr. Schucman in 1975 for this purpose. This Combined Volume also includes the supplements to the *Course:* Psychotherapy: Purpose, Process and Practice and The Song of Prayer. These sections are extensions of the *Course* principles, which were dictated to Dr. Schucman shortly after she completed *A Course in Miracles.*

The Foundation for Inner Peace may be contacted through their website or by mail:

Foundation for Inner Peace
P.O. Box 598
Mill Valley, CA 94942-0598
www.acim.org

ABOUT THE AUTHOR

Gary R. Renard underwent a powerful spiritual awakening in the early 1990s. As instructed by two ascended masters who appeared to him in the flesh, he wrote his first best-selling book, *The Disappearance of the Universe,* over a period of nine years. He was later guided to speak in public and has been described as one of the most interesting and courageous spiritual speakers in the world. Gary's second book, *Your Immortal Reality,* was also a bestseller.

Over the past ten years, Gary has spoken in 43 states and 24 countries, and was the keynote speaker at the International *A Course in Miracles* Conferences in Salt Lake City, San Francisco, and Chicago. He is also a recipient of the Infinity Foundation Spirit Award, which is given to those who have made a meaningful contribution to personal and spiritual growth. Past recipients include Dan Millman, Ram Dass, Gary Zukav, James Redfield, Byron Katie, and Neale Donald Walsch.

More recently, Gary has been busy teaching (and sometimes introducing) *A Course in Miracles* with talks and workshops all over the world. He has done hundreds of radio and print interviews; appeared in seven documentary movies; recorded 47 podcasts with Gene Bogart; posted 30 videos on YouTube; created three audio CDs for Sounds True (one of which has over seven hours of unedited material); made a music CD and a meditation CD with Cindy Lora-Renard; filmed several DVDs; gone through a divorce; moved from Maine to California; gotten married again; created a television series based on his books; written the pilot script (along with Elysia Skye) for the TV series, plus a seven-year treatment for the show; answered thousands of e-mails; written the Forewords for seven books; developed the largest *A Course in Miracles* study group in the world (The D.U. Discussion Group at Yahoo); had his book published in 21 languages, including on Mainland China . . . and he has now begun to make more time for writing. Because of this, new books are expected in the future.

Website: www.GaryRenard.com

NOTES

NOTES

NOTES

Hay House Titles of Related Interest

YOU CAN HEAL YOUR LIFE, the movie,
starring Louise Hay & Friends
(available as an online streaming video)
www.hayhouse.com/louise-movie

THE SHIFT, the movie,
starring Dr. Wayne W. Dyer
(available as an online streaming video)
www.hayhouse.com/the-shift-movie

THE AMAZING POWER OF DELIBERATE INTENT:
Living the Art of Allowing, by Esther and Jerry Hicks
(The Teachings of Abraham®)

ARCHANGELS & ASCENDED MASTERS: A Guide to Working
and Healing with Divinities and Deities, by Doreen Virtue

GRACE, GAIA, AND THE END OF DAYS: An Alternative
Way for the Advanced Soul, by Stuart Wilde

THE HIDDEN POWER OF YOUR PAST LIVES: Revealing
Your Encoded Consciousness, by Sandra Anne Taylor

LOYALTY TO YOUR SOUL: The Heart of Spiritual Psychology,
by H. Ronald Hulnick, Ph.D., and Mary R. Hulnick, Ph.D.

THE POWER OF INFINITE LOVE & GRATITUDE,
by Dr. Darren R. Weissman

SPOKEN MIRACLES:
A Companion to The Disappearance of the Universe,
by Martha Lucía Espinosa

All of the above are available at your local bookstore,
or may be ordered by contacting Hay House (see next page).

or may be ordered by contacting Hay House (see next page).

We hope you enjoyed this Hay House book. If you'd like to receive
our online catalog featuring additional information on Hay House
books and products, or if you'd like to find out more about the
Hay Foundation, please contact:

Hay House, Inc., P.O. Box 5100, Carlsbad, CA 92018-5100
(760) 431-7695 or (800) 654-5126
(760) 431-6948 (fax) or (800) 650-5115 (fax)
www.hayhouse.com® • www.hayfoundation.org

———

Published in Australia by: Hay House Australia Pty. Ltd.,
18/36 Ralph St., Alexandria NSW 2015
Phone: 612-9669-4299 • *Fax:* 612-9669-4144
www.hayhouse.com.au

Published in the United Kingdom by: Hay House UK, Ltd.,
The Sixth Floor, Watson House, 54 Baker Street, London W1U 7BU
Phone: +44 (0)20 3927 7290 • *Fax:* +44 (0)20 3927 7291
www.hayhouse.co.uk

Published in India by: Hay House Publishers India,
Muskaan Complex, Plot No. 3, B-2, Vasant Kunj, New Delhi 110 070
Phone: 91-11-4176-1620 • *Fax:* 91-11-4176-1630
www.hayhouse.co.in

———

Access New Knowledge.
Anytime. Anywhere.

Learn and evolve at your own pace
with the world's leading experts.

www.hayhouseU.com

Printed in the United States
by Baker & Taylor Publisher Services